WALKING IN THE
NORTH WESSEX DOWNS

WALKING IN THE
NORTH WESSEX DOWNS

30 WALKS EXPLORING THE AONB

by Steve Davison

JUNIPER HOUSE, MURLEY MOSS,
OXENHOLME ROAD, KENDAL, CUMBRIA LA9 7RL
www.cicerone.co.uk

© Steve Davison 2021
Second edition 2021
ISBN: 978 1 78631 110 8
First edition 2015

Printed in Czechia on responsibly sourced paper on behalf of Latitude Press Ltd.
A catalogue record for this book is available from the British Library.
All photographs are by the author unless otherwise stated.

© Crown copyright 2021. OS PU100012932.

Acknowledgements

*The author would like to thank Tim Lewis, for help in checking the accuracy of
the walks in this guidebook.*

CITY AND COUNTY OF SWANSEA LIBRARIES

6000397614

Askews & Holts	09-Dec-2021
796.51	£12.95
SWCL	

Front cover: Mystical Silbury Hill at Avebury (Walk 18)

CONTENTS

Route symbols on OS map extracts
(for OS legend see printed OS maps)

route

alternative route

(🚶) start/finish point

(🚶) alternative start/finish point

◀ route direction

```
0                          1km
|-------------|-------------|
0                       0.5 mile
```

The extracts from 1:50,000 OS maps
used in this book have been reproduced
at 1:40,000 for greater clarity

Features on the overview map

——— County/Unitary boundary

Urban area

Area of Outstanding Natural
Beauty/National Scenic Area
eg *North Wessex Downs*

600m
400m
200m
75m
0m

GPX files
GPX files for all routes can be downloaded
for free at www.cicerone.co.uk/1110/gpx

The fascinating linear earthwork of the Wansdyke stretches out across Tan Hill (Walk 21)

The Devil's Den – three large sarsen stones seen on Walk 17

INTRODUCTION

Looking north across The Manger and the Vale of White Horse from the Uffington White Horse (Walk 11)

The North Wessex Downs Area of Outstanding Natural Beauty (AONB), the third largest AONB in England, covers an area of 1730km² and takes in parts of four counties – Berkshire, Hampshire, Oxfordshire and Wiltshire. It encompasses one of the largest and least developed tracts of chalk downland in southern England. The AONB has a relatively low population, but because its boundary skirts around larger urban areas, such as Swindon, Reading and Basingstoke, a large number of people live within easy access.

This rolling chalk down-land stretches west from the River Thames in a broad arc to the south of Swindon, including the Berkshire and Marlborough Downs, with a steep scarp slope looking out over the Vale of White Horse, and then sweeps south and east to include the Vale of Pewsey and the North Hampshire Downs before circling round Newbury back to the Thames.

Although the downs are termed 'hilly', they don't rise to any great height, which makes the walks here suitable for a wide range of abilities. Nevertheless, the walks in this guide take in not only the highest chalk hill in England (and highest point in Berkshire), Walbury Hill (297m;

Walk 26), but also the highest points in three other counties – Milk Hill in Wiltshire (294m; Walk 21), Pilot Hill in Hampshire (286m; Walk 27) and Whitehorse Hill in Oxfordshire (261m; Walk 11).

This classic chalk landscape has been shaped by human activity for thousands of years, and some of the walks follow ancient trackways past some stunning historic sites, such as Avebury (one of the largest henge monuments in Britain; Walk 18), the 3000-year-old stylised galloping figure of the Uffington White Horse (Walk 11), impressive Neolithic long barrows, Bronze Age barrows and Iron Age hill forts. Take time to admire the views and ponder why and how our ancestors created these iconic features.

But that's not all. The walks allow you to explore parts of the Ridgeway National Trail, the Kennet and Avon Canal, peaceful riverside locations and picture-postcard villages with thatched cottages, historic churches and cosy pubs.

The North Wessex Downs offer an abundance of peace and tranquillity – here you can listen to skylarks singing over the open chalk grassland and the wind gently rustling through the trees; be dazzled by the myriad of flowers and butterflies; in late autumn see flocks of fieldfares and redwings feed along the hedgerows; and enjoy the views across the gently rolling chalk landscape that has inspired many a writer, poet and artist over the years.

For more information on this beautiful area, see www.northwessex downs.org.uk.

GEOLOGY

The geology of the North Wessex Downs tells the story of the seas that once covered southern England and the sediments that were laid down at that time. The predominant feature – one that forms the rolling contours of the downs – is a thick layer of Upper Cretaceous chalk (99–65 million years old), composed of incredible numbers of tiny fossil skeletons of algae, called coccoliths. Associated with the upper (white) layer of chalk are horizontal bands of irregular silica concretions, known as flints. These also occur in profusion in the jumbled deposits of weathered chalk, known as 'clay-with-flints'. When struck, flint breaks with a shell-shaped fracture, leaving very sharp edges, and our Stone Age ancestors used flints to make arrowheads and hand axes. Being a very

Upper (white) chalk with layer of flint

hard-wearing rock, flint has also been widely used as a building material.

Underlying the porous chalk is an impervious layer of Gault Clay laid down during the latter part of the Lower Cretaceous period (145–99 million years ago). This junction between the clay and chalk gives rise to the spring-line along the northern edges of the downs, where water that has seeped through the chalk is forced to the surface to form springs.

A natural process of patchy and irregular hardening within the sandy beds that overlay the chalk produced blocks of tough sandstone that are more resistant to erosion. These are the famous sarsens, known locally as grey wethers (from a distance they are said to resemble sheep – a 'wether' being a castrated ram). Sarsens were used in the construction of the stone circle at Avebury and the Neolithic long barrows at West Kennett (Walk 18) and Wayland's Smithy (Walk 11); a great number of sarsens can be seen in their natural state at Fyfield Down National Nature Reserve (Walk 17).

Throughout the last 2.6 million years (the Quaternary period) Britain has been subject to periods of glaciation separated by warmer interglacial periods (the last glacial period ended about 12,000 years ago). There is no evidence to suggest that the North Wessex Downs were ever covered in ice, but the area did suffer periglacial conditions that allowed the

Wilton Windmill – the only working windmill within the North Wessex Downs (passed on Walk 24)

formation of dry valleys, or coombes, in the chalk plateau. The coombes were formed by erosion, as water flowed over the surface of the chalk during cold periods when the underlying ground was frozen, making the normally porous chalk impermeable (good examples of coombes are seen on Walks 10, 11 and 12).

Another major feature caused by glaciation was the creation of the Goring Gap, through which the River Thames now flows. The gap was created when a large glacial lake, which formed over the Oxford area about 450,000 years ago, eroded a line of weakness in the chalk. The Goring Gap now forms a junction between the Berkshire Downs to the west and the Chiltern Hills to the east.

BRIEF HISTORY

The earliest inhabitants of the area were nomadic hunter-gatherers who travelled through the wooded landscape over 10,000 years ago. However, by the Neolithic period (4200–2200BC) a farming lifestyle was developing, permanent camps were being constructed, and areas of land cleared for crops and animals. This is the period when the great monuments at Avebury came into being. The Bronze Age (2200–750BC) saw further developments at Avebury, as well as the building of numerous characteristic round barrows. It was during this period, some 3000 years ago, that the stylised galloping outline of the Uffington White Horse was carved into the chalk. Later, during

The Kennet and Avon Canal (Walk 21)

Monument to Colonel Robert Loyd-Lindsay, soldier and philanthropist (Walk 6)

the Iron Age (750BC–AD43), defensive hill forts such as Barbury Castle (Walk 16) were built.

The Romans left little visible evidence in the region, although they did construct several roads that are still used today. Archaeological investigations have shown that they built a fortified town near Mildenhall (Walk 14) and a number of villas, including one near Ramsbury (Walk 13).

The demise of the Roman Empire in Britain around AD410 was followed by a Saxon invasion. In AD556 Saxons led by Cynric and his son Ceawlin (who later became King of Wessex in AD560) defeated the Britons at the Battle of Beranburgh (Beran Byrig);

the site of the battle is claimed to be Barbury Castle (Walk 16). It was during the early part of the Saxon period that the Wansdyke – a massive linear earthwork across the Marlborough Downs – was constructed (Walk 21).

During the ninth century Danes were invading parts of England, and in AD871 Alfred the Great, who was born at Wantage, defeated the Danes at the Battle of Ashdown in Berkshire ('Ashdown' was the ancient name for the whole expanse of the Berkshire Downs). He later became King of Wessex and Overlord of England, funded church schools, brought in a code of laws and developed his capital at Winchester, where he is buried.

The Norman period, following the Battle of Hastings in 1066, was the time of the Domesday Book, when many motte and bailey castles were built, along with monasteries and churches characterised by Romanesque rounded arches over windows and doorways. Many churches within the North Wessex Downs have their roots in the Norman period.

Prosperity and growth in the late 12th and the 13th centuries led to the expansion of towns surrounding the downs. In the 18th and 19th centuries, transport improved with the opening of the Kennet and Avon Canal, quickly followed by the arrival of the railways. During the Second World War a number of airfields were built, including Wroughton and Alton Barnes.

Major transport connections in the area, such as the opening of the M4 and A34, have allowed towns and villages to continue to grow, but this has put more pressure on precious countryside. However, in 1972 much of the rolling chalk countryside was designated an Area of Outstanding Natural Beauty, and this should help to preserve this special area for future generations.

PLANTS AND WILDLIFE

The North Wessex Downs form a patchwork landscape with areas of open chalk grassland, broad-leaved woodland and farmland. Chalk streams flow from the spring-line that forms along the boundary between the upper porous chalk and the lower impervious layer of clay, where water that has seeped through the porous layer is forced to the surface. Chalk streams support a diversity of plant and animal life. Some of these streams in their upper reaches

Common blue butterfly (Polyommatus icarus) *(L); Small heath butterfly* (Coenonympha pamphilus) *(R)*

Clockwise from left: Harebell (Campanula rotundifolia); *Clustered bellflower*
(Campanula glomerata); Autumn gentian (Gentianella amarella)

are termed 'winterbournes', and appear only after sustained heavy winter rainfall, such as the River Lambourn between Lambourn and East Garston.

Throughout the region there should be plenty of opportunities for catching glimpses of local wildlife, from foxes to roe and fallow deer (or the much smaller muntjac) – and perhaps even the elusive badger as dusk approaches.

The open chalk grasslands support a wide range of butterflies, plants (including gentians and orchids) and birds, such as the skylark and yellow-hammer. High above, you might see the silhouette of a buzzard or hear the high-pitched whistling call of a red kite, with its distinctive forked tail and chestnut-red plumage.

Alongside the streams and rivers, as well as the ever-present ducks and mute swans, there may be glimpses of the vivid turquoise-blue-and-orange flash of a kingfisher as it darts along the river, or of an otter or the endangered water vole.

15

WHERE TO STAY

The North Wessex Downs has a wide range of accommodation ranging from youth hostels and campsites to pubs with rooms, guesthouses and hotels. To find out more about accommodation, visit the tourist information websites listed in Appendix B.

GETTING AROUND

Major roads passing through the North Wessex Downs include the M4, A4 and A34. If travelling by car to any of the walks always remember to park considerately and never block access routes.

Rail stations that provide access to the North Wessex Downs include Didcot, Goring and Streatley, Great Bedwyn, Hungerford, Kintbury, Newbury, Pewsey and Swindon. The majority of the walks are accessible by public transport, and brief information is provided in the box at the start of each walk. However, most bus services do not operate on Sundays, and some services are quite limited. Only a few of the walks can be accessed by train, and a note of the nearest station is given in the box at the start of these walks. For the latest information relating to public transport use the contact details in Appendix B.

FOOD AND DRINK

Food and drink may be bought at the start of some walks (at a shop, café or pub), while others offer opportunities for stopping off en route at a pub or shop – although these are not always

The Bell Inn at Aldworth (Walk 3)

conveniently placed along the route. Brief details of refreshment opportunities are given in the information box at the start of each walk, but bear in mind that there is no guarantee they'll be open when required. It's therefore always a good idea to carry some food and drink with you, along with a small 'emergency ration' in case of an unexpected delay.

LONG-DISTANCE ROUTES

A number of long-distance paths run through the North Wessex Downs AONB, including significant sections of the Lambourn Valley Way and the Ridgeway. Some of these paths intersect with walks in this guide (see below), and offer the opportunity for walkers to create their own longer route.

- **Lambourn Valley Way** A 32km (20 mile) route from the Ridgeway at the Whitehorse Hill car park along the Lambourn Valley to Newbury, passing through Lambourn, Eastbury, East Garston, Great Shefford and Boxford. Crosses Walks 8 and 9.
- **Ridgeway National Trail** The southern section of the trail from Overton Hill near Avebury to the River Thames at Streatley travels for 68km (42¼ miles) along the northern scarp of the North Wessex Downs. Crosses Walks 3, 5, 6, 10, 11, 12, 16, 17 and 18.
- **Test Way** Follows the Test Valley from Eling Wharf on the outskirts

of Southampton to end at Inkpen Beacon (73km/45 miles). Crosses Walks 26 and 28.
- **Wayfarer's Walk** A route through Hampshire from Inkpen Beacon to Emsworth (114km/71 miles). Crosses Walks 26, 27, 29 and 30.
- **White Horse Trail** A route visiting all eight white-horse hill figures within Wiltshire, seven of which are within the North Wessex Downs (145km/90 miles). Crosses Walks 15, 16, 17 and 18, 19, 20, 21 and 23.
- **Sarsen Way** A route from Barbury Castle to Old Sarum, with detours to Avebury, Stonehenge and Salisbury (58.5km/36 miles or 85.7km/53 miles). Crosses Walks 17, 18 and 21.
- **Brenda Parker Way** A 126km (78 mile) route developed by the North Hampshire Ramblers Group running between Andover and Aldershot. Crosses Walks 27 and 28.

MAPS

The Ordnance Survey (OS) offer two series of maps – the 1:50,000 (2cm to 1km) Landranger series and the more detailed 1:25,000 (4cm to 1km) Explorer series. The OS maps covering the North Wessex Downs AONB are:
- Landranger: 173, 174, 175 and 185
- Explorer: 130, 131, 144, 157, 158, 159 and 170

Memorial stone on Walbury Hill (Walk 26) to soldiers who trained here in 1944

This guide features extracts of the OS 1:50,000 Landranger series of maps, increased to 1:40,000 for greater clarity, with overlays showing the route, along with any detours or short-cuts. It is advisable to always carry the relevant Explorer map with you when walking.

WALKING IN THE NORTH WESSEX DOWNS

The walks in this guide range from 6.4 to 20.6km (4 to 12¾ miles) and cover fairly low-level terrain (below 297m), and although some have several, sometimes steep, climbs and descents, they should be suitable for most walkers. The routes follow well-defined tracks and paths, although some follow narrow, and at times indistinct, paths – especially through woods, where careful navigation may be required.

As for the weather, summers tend to be fairly dry and mild. Spring and autumn offer some of the best walking conditions – spring and early summer herald new life in the North Wessex Downs with colourful displays of flowers, abundant birdsong and many butterflies, while cool autumn nights clothe the countryside in shades of russet, gold and brown. During the winter months, spells of rain can make some routes quite muddy. However, walking on a clear, frosty winter's day can be a magical experience.

Always choose clothing suitable for the season, along with a waterproof jacket, comfortable and waterproof footwear and a comfortable rucksack. On wet days gaiters or waterproof trousers can also be very useful. It's also worth carrying a basic first aid kit to deal with minor incidents.

Make every effort to avoid disturbing the wildlife and keep dogs under close control at all times. Finally, always take care when either walking along or crossing roads.

WAYMARKING, ACCESS AND RIGHTS OF WAY

Rights of way throughout the North Wessex Downs are typically well signposted using a mix of fingerposts, marker posts and waymarks on fences and gateposts. The descriptions in this guide, in combination with the map extracts and the signage on the ground, should make route finding straightforward; however, it is still advisable to carry the relevant OS Explorer map and a compass.

The walks in this guide follow official rights of way, whether that is footpaths, bridleways, restricted byways or byways. Some routes also pass areas of open access land (marked on OS Explorer maps) where walkers can freely roam.

Rights of way are indicated on signage as follows:
- **Footpaths** yellow arrow – walkers only
- **Bridleways** blue arrow – walkers, cyclists and horse riders
- **Restricted byways** purple arrow – walkers, cyclists, horse riders and carriage drivers
- **Byways** red arrow – same as for a restricted byway plus motorcycles and motorised vehicles

PROTECTING THE COUNTRYSIDE

When out walking, please respect the countryside and follow the Countryside Code:
- Be safe – plan ahead and follow any signs
- Leave gates and property as you find them
- Protect plants and animals, and take your litter home
- Keep dogs under close control
- Consider other people

Rights of way are usually well signposted

Many of the walks pass through fields where cattle may be present. Follow the latest advice – do not walk between cows and young calves; if you feel threatened move away calmly – do not panic or make sudden noises; if possible find an alternative route.

USING THIS GUIDE

This guide is divided into five sections, starting with walks in the eastern half of the Berkshire Downs. It then heads west through West Berkshire to cover the Lambourn Downs. Continuing west, and crossing into Wiltshire, the next two sections describe walks in the Marlborough Downs and, to the south, the Vale of Pewsey. The final walks are in the North Hampshire Downs, tucked into the upper western corner of Hampshire.

The route descriptions all follow the same format. The information box gives the start/finish location accompanied by a grid reference and brief parking details (if parking is limited, details of any alternative parking/ start points are also given here); walk distance (kilometres/miles); ascent (metres); minimum walk time; relevant map details; places that offer refreshments (pubs, cafés and shops); and brief public transport information.

This is followed by a short introduction to the route, identifying any major points of interest, including villages. The route is then described in detail, with background information

on features or places of interest given in green paragraphs and boxes.

The map extracts are from the 1:50,000 OS Landranger series, increased to 1:40,000 for greater clarity. Key features on the map that are also mentioned in the route are highlighted in **bold** to help with route finding.

The route summary table in Appendix A provides the key statistics for all the walks. Appendix B lists contact points for further information that may be useful when planning walks or a stay in the area. Finally, a selection of books that provide interesting further reading on the region are given in Appendix C.

Times and distances

The distances quoted for each walk – metric first, with approximate imperial conversions rounded to the nearest ¼, ½, ¾ or whole number – have been measured from OS Explorer maps. Note that the heights given on the maps are in metres and the grid lines are spaced at intervals of 1km. The walking time for each walk has been worked out using a walking speed of 4km/hr (2½ miles/ hr), plus 10 minutes for every 100m of ascent. This should be treated as the **minimum** amount of walking time required to undertake the walk. It does not include any time for rests, photography, consulting the map or guidebook, or simply admiring the view – all of which can add substantially to the day's activity.

BERKSHIRE DOWNS EAST

The first part of Walk 3 follows a section of the Ridgeway

WALK 1

Chapel Row, Bucklebury and Stanford Dingley

Start/finish	Junction of The Avenue and Hatch Lane at Chapel Row (SU 571 696); limited parking. Alternative parking/start: Bucklebury recreation ground (SU 552 708)
Distance	11.6km (7¼ miles)
Ascent	230m
Time	3¼hr
Map	OS Explorer 158
Refreshments	Blackbird Café (0118 9712332) and The Bladebone (0118 9714000) at Chapel Row; The Pot Kiln (01635 201366) at Frilsham; The Bull Inn (0118 9744582) and The Old Boot Inn (0118 9745191) at Stanford Dingley
Public transport	Bus services to Chapel Row from Newbury and Tilehurst (excluding Sundays)

After leaving Chapel Row the route heads down towards the River Pang and the picturesque village of Bucklebury before meandering through woods to the ideally located Pot Kiln pub. The return continues through woods and open fields to call in at peaceful Stanford Dingley before a gradual ascent back to Chapel Row.

From **Chapel Row** head west along the main road (Thatcham direction), passing The Bladebone pub, and after 250m turn right across the road. Follow the track, signposted to Scotland Corner, through the trees of Chapelrow Common.

Keep left at the split to a junction and turn left for 50m to another junction just after passing a house (right). Turn right and follow the bridleway down through the trees – keeping right at a bridleway junction – to a lane. Turn left up the lane for 100m, and just after passing a house turn right over a stile in the hedge. Head northwards down through the field with a view across the

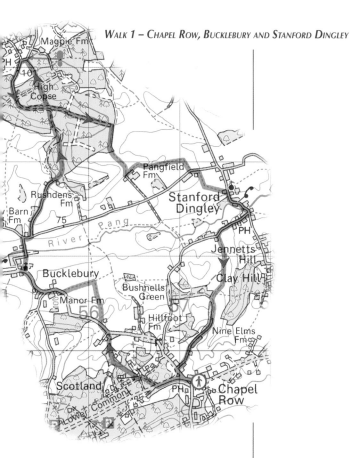

valley and cross a stile in the lower-right corner. Keep ahead through the next field following the left-hand margin to a four-way path junction beside a footbridge. Do not cross the footbridge, but turn left along the grass strip between fields aiming for the large house.

Cross a stile and turn right along the lane passing **Manor Farm**, keeping right at the junction towards **Bucklebury**. After the Old Vicarage turn right, following the surfaced path through the churchyard and passing clockwise round St Mary's Church. ▶ Go through gates

The alternative parking/start is up the road ahead at the junction.

23

either side of a track and continue across the field before leaving through a gate.

> The **manor of Bucklebury**, mentioned in the Domesday Book, was granted to Reading Abbey by Henry I. Following Henry VIII's Dissolution of the Monasteries, the manor was sold to John Winchcombe, son of the famous 'Jack of Newbury' who had made his wealth in the cloth trade.
>
> The 11th-century parish Church of **St Mary the Virgin** has some impressive features, including an elaborately carved Norman doorway. The colourful east window depicting the Crucifixion, by Sir Frank Brangwyn, is unusual in that the crucified Christ is looking up to heaven, rather than down at the ground. Before leaving, take a look at the curious 'fly-window', complete with painted sundial; the realistic fly is a pictorial substitute for the usual sun-dial motto – *Tempus fugit* ('time flies').

Follow the road northwards, crossing the **River Pang**, to a junction. Turn right towards Stanford Dingley for 75m before going left up a lane signposted to Old Hawkridge House and Cottage.

At the brick-and-timber house keep right towards a gated (private) entrance and then fork left onto a narrow restricted byway up through the trees with a fence on the right (ignore paths to the left and right). Continue up through Burgess' Copse, passing over the brow of the hill, then down to a dip and back up before reaching a signposted crossing track at SU 556 725. ◄

Cross over and follow the narrow path down through the trees of **High Copse**, ignoring a crossing track (private). Go through a gate and follow the right-hand boundary through two fields, separated by a footbridge and gate. Leave through a gate in the top-right corner and turn left along the lane to the Pot Kiln pub. At one time there were a number of kilns here that were used to fire bricks made from local clay deposits; much later the West Berkshire Brewery (now in Yattendon, Walk 2)

Anyone not wanting to visit the Pot Kiln pub at Frilsham can turn right here to continue with the walk (1.5km shorter route).

started brewing in one of the old barns. Continue along the lane up to a right-hand bend and fork left along the track. Keep right (straight on) at the split and follow the track as it curves left back to the junction passed earlier; keep ahead.

Follow the track eastwards for 700m, through the wood (passing Highwood Copse) and later descending to a junction. Turn right along the tree-shaded byway for 500m to reach a track; the restricted byway goes straight on through the trees.

Here, turn left and follow the track (permissive path) as it curves right along the field edge towards **Pangfield Farm**. Stay in the field and turn left following the right-hand boundary through two fields. Go through a gate in the corner beside some trees and keep ahead through the next field, following the boundary on the left along two sides of the field to a lane.

Turn left along the lane for 100m then right up the bank and follow the right-hand field edge. Cross two

Following a good track past Highwood Copse

St Denys' Church

stiles and bear half-left across two fields separated by a stile aiming for the church in **Stanford Dingley**. Cross a stile in the field corner and turn right along the lane.

The name of picturesque **Stanford Dingley** is derived from the original lord of the manor, William de Stanford, mentioned in 1224, and from the Dyneley family, who lived here in the Middle Ages. The church here is unusual in that it is dedicated to St Denys, who was martyred in third-century France. The church has Saxon origins, although it mostly dates from the 12th and 13th centuries, with a 15th-century white weather-boarded bell turret. Inside there are fragments of 13th-century wall paintings, a brass memorial to Margaret Dyneley dated 1444, and a modern engraved memorial window to the novelist and poet Robert Gathorne-Hardy (1902–1973), who lived in the village for many years.

Follow the lane and, once level with The Bull Inn, fork right across the grass to follow an enclosed path, soon crossing the River Pang beside the former mill (private house) to join a road beside the tile-hung Garden House. Turn right along the road for 400m, soon passing The Old Boot Inn. At the right-hand bend, just before some houses, turn left along a track (bridleway). Enter a field and follow the right-hand boundary to the top-right corner. Go through a gate and follow the bridleway uphill with trees to the right. Continue up along the track passing St Crispins Farm to a road. Turn left and keep left at the junction to get back to the start.

The Bull Inn

WALK 2

Ashampstead and Yattendon

Start/finish	North edge of the recreation ground in Ashampstead (SU 565 769); limited roadside parking
Distance	6.9km (4¼ miles)
Ascent	65m
Time	2hr
Map	OS Explorer 158
Refreshments	Casey Fields Farm Shop (01635 579662) at Ashampstead; The Royal Oak (01635 201325) and village shop at Yattendon
Public transport	None

This easy walk meanders through fairly level farmland and visits two interesting villages, Ashampstead and Yattendon. Step inside St Clement's Church near the start of the walk to see its medieval wall paintings, while the Church of St Peter and St Paul at Yattendon is the resting place of a poet laureate. Yattendon is also home to the award-winning West Berkshire Brewery.

Stand facing the large green in **Ashampstead** and turn right to a crossroads. Go left down Church Lane for 100m before turning right through a gate to enter the churchyard. Follow the path passing just left of St Clement's Church, and leave the churchyard through a gate on the western boundary.

Ashampstead dates back to at least the time of the Norman Conquest, when William the Conqueror gave the lands to William FitzOsborn. St Clement's Church dates from the late 12th century, with later additions. The church contains a real treasure – surviving fragments of 13th-century medieval wall paintings. Those on the north wall of the nave depict scenes from the birth of Christ, while on the chancel arch can be seen the remains of the

Last Judgement, with the figures of Christ and the Apostles and souls being admitted to heaven (left) or dragged down to hell (right). The paintings were uncovered only in 1895, having been plastered over following the Reformation in the 16th century.

Medieval wall paintings inside St Clement's Church, Ashampstead

Head west across two fields separated by a gate and turn left along the concrete track (bridle-way). Just before Casey Fields Farm Shop turn right following a track through trees. Enter a field and keep ahead with trees on the right for 175m to a marker post. Turn left across the field, passing just left of a solitary tree to the trees on the far side.

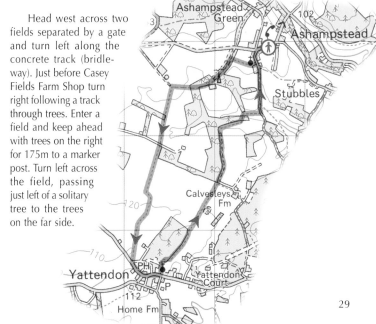

29

The Royal Oak at Yattendon

Keep ahead through a gate and follow the left-hand field edge. Cross a track and continue between the trees (left) and hedge (right). Go through another gate and follow the hedge on the right. At the field corner turn left for 75m, still following the hedge, and then turn right through a gate.

Head diagonally left across the corner of the field, cross the boundary into the next field and turn right following the right-hand field margin for 200m. At the marker post head diagonally left across the field, passing a wooden electricity pole and tree mid field. Go through a gate, continue through the small paddock and leave through another gate. Bear left up the road to a junction in **Yattendon** beside The Royal Oak, with the village store opposite.

Like Ashampstead, picturesque **Yattendon** was mentioned in the Domesday Book, when the manor was held by 'William son of Ansculf'. Inside the 15th-century Church of St Peter and St Paul is a memorial to Sir John Norreys (d.1466), a distinguished soldier in the reign of Elizabeth I and lord of the manor who built the present church; the Norreys family, and their descendants, held the manor of Yattendon until the 19th century. On the north wall of the nave there is a tablet (Latin inscription) commemorating Harriet Molesworth, her son Robert Seymour Bridges (1844–1930) and his wife Monica Waterhouse. Robert Bridges, a doctor by profession, became poet laureate in 1913; his works include 'London snow' (1879).

The village is also home to the award-winning West Berkshire Brewery, originally established in 1995 in a barn at the Pot Kiln pub (Walk 1). The brewery and shop are located 400m south of the church along Church Lane and then left along Chapel Lane (SU 554 741).

Keep left past The Royal Oak, and 50m after passing the village hall turn left through a gate to enter the churchyard. Follow the path through the churchyard, passing just left of the Church of St Peter and St Paul before leaving through a gate in the far right corner.

Turn right along the path and head north-eastwards between trees (left) and a hedge (right); the woods have a good display of bluebells in late spring. At the end of the wood keep ahead through the field for 600m following the right-hand boundary to a crossing track; **Calvesleys Farm** is to the right. Keep ahead, now with a wood on the left and open field to the right. At the corner follow the field edge round to the right for 250m. Shortly before the next field corner, turn left at the marker post and head north-east down through the trees to a track. Turn right (east) along the track following the valley floor to a crossing track – Pinfold Lane.

Turn left up the track back to Ashampstead, later following Church Lane past St Clement's Church and turning right at the crossroads to get back to the start.

WALK 3
Aldworth

Start/finish	Ridgeway car park at end of Rectory Road off the A417 at Streatley (SU 567 812)
Distance	8.8km (5½ miles)
Ascent	170m
Time	2½hr
Maps	OS Explorer 159 and 170
Refreshments	The Bell Inn (01635 578272) at Aldworth
Public transport	Streatley (off route, accessible by following the waymarked Ridgeway for 2km) has bus links to Reading (excluding Sundays); Goring and Streatley station has good rail links (3.5km off route)

This easy half-day walk follows a short section of the Ridgeway, meandering through the Berkshire Downs just west of the River Thames with views of the Chilterns. The high point of the walk is the picturesque village of Aldworth, a place where giants sleep, before a gradual descent leads back to the start.

Inside St Mary's Church is the large effigy of Sir Nicholas de la Beche

From car park, head west up the track following the Ridgeway for 1.7km to a track junction. Turn left along the track, with a view to the east across Streatley Warren to the Chilterns, and then follow the track as it swings right to a surfaced lane. Turn left along the lane for 250m and then right down a track, following it as it swings left at the trees to pass Dumworth Farm to join a road beside St Mary's Church in **Aldworth**.

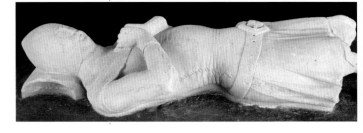

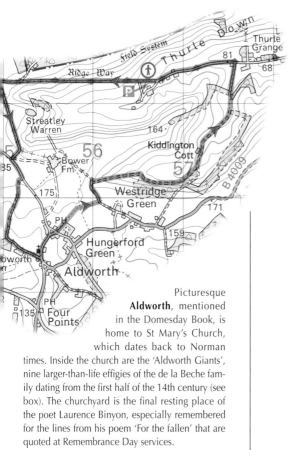

Picturesque **Aldworth**, mentioned in the Domesday Book, is home to St Mary's Church, which dates back to Norman times. Inside the church are the 'Aldworth Giants', nine larger-than-life effigies of the de la Beche family dating from the first half of the 14th century (see box). The churchyard is the final resting place of the poet Laurence Binyon, especially remembered for the lines from his poem 'For the fallen' that are quoted at Remembrance Day services.

Turn left and keep right at the split to reach The Bell Inn. ▶ Turn right along the road for 20m, and then go left along the enclosed path. Continue across the field, go through the hedge, ignore the crossing path and continue ahead (eastwards) across the field. Turn left along the track for 250m to a signed junction and turn right.

Follow the track (footpath) downhill, go through the hedge into the next field and bear slightly right to follow the field edge with Westridge Copse on the right, heading east. At the end of the wood bear left and head north

Opposite the inn is a canopied well said to be one of the deepest in England at 111m.

THE ALDWORTH GIANTS

The influential de la Beche family, many of whom were warders of the Tower of London and Sheriffs of Oxfordshire and Berkshire, had come to England in the wake of William the Conqueror and built the long-since vanished 'castle' of de la Beche nearby. A silver seal bearing the name Isabella de la Beche was found in 1871 and is now held in Reading Museum.

According to tradition four of the family effigies, or giants, in the church were known by other names – the largest was known as John Long, and the three others as John Strong, John Never Afraid and John Ever Afraid. The last of the three, whose effigy has disappeared, is said to have promised his soul to the Devil in exchange for worldly riches, 'whether he was buried inside or outside the church'. However, at his death he tricked the Devil by being buried in the wall, neither in nor out of the church. The arch where the statue lay is on the outside of the south wall.

Although the effigies have suffered some damage over the centuries, probably during the English Civil War, they are still an impressive sight and constitute the largest number of medieval memorials to a single family in a parish church.

After passing through Aldworth the route heads back towards the Ridgeway, with distant views of the Chilterns

towards **Kiddington Cottage**, partly hidden by trees. Continue along the track, passing to the right of the house, and keep to the track as it curves right, heading north-east between fields. Later fork right to follow a parallel path through the trees and then rejoin the track. Keep ahead along the enclosed track to join a lane (this is also the Ridgeway National Trail) beside a house, and turn left for 900m back to the car park (right leads to Streatley).

WALK 4

Shillingford, Wittenham Clumps
and Dorchester on Thames

Start/finish	Henley Road (A4074) in Shillingford, just north-west of the roundabout (SU 595 928); limited roadside parking
Distance	13.2km (8¼ miles)
Ascent	190m
Time	3¾hr
Map	OS Explorer 170
Refreshments	The Red Lion (01491 837373) at Brightwell-cum-Sotwell; pubs, tea room and shop at Dorchester on Thames
Public transport	Daily bus services to Shillingford from Oxford and Reading

From Shillingford the walk soon crosses the River Thames to call in at Brightwell-cum-Sotwell, with its picturesque thatched cottages. From here it's off to the distinctive twin tree-crowned tops of the Wittenham Clumps, tucked in the far north-east corner of the North Wessex Downs, from where there is a great view. The walk then drops down to historic Dorchester on Thames before heading back alongside the River Thames.

Head north-west from the lay-by in **Shillingford** to the crossroads and turn left along Wharf Road (Thames Path). Near the end turn left along the enclosed Thames Path, keep right, cross the drive to Shillingford Court, and later bear left along the surfaced track to a road. Turn right across the **River Thames**, then right again just before the Shillingford Bridge Hotel.

Continue through the car park, follow the track towards North Farm for 50m and turn left up through the trees. Continue across two fields, passing a wooden electricity pole, and at the bridleway junction bear left towards the trees. Continue down through the wood (sunken route) for 300m, and then fork right on a path with a fence on the left. Then follow the left-hand field margin to the corner.

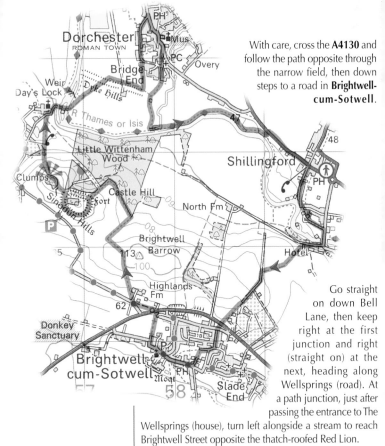

With care, cross the **A4130** and follow the path opposite through the narrow field, then down steps to a road in **Brightwell-cum-Sotwell**.

Go straight on down Bell Lane, then keep right at the first junction and right (straight on) at the next, heading along Wellsprings (road). At a path junction, just after passing the entrance to The Wellsprings (house), turn left alongside a stream to reach Brightwell Street opposite the thatch-roofed Red Lion.

Turn right through the village, later passing The Square (with war memorial), and keep ahead along West End passing the brick-and-flint Stewart Memorial Hall and clock tower built in memory of a former rector, the Revd John Haldane Stewart. ◀ Follow the road as it swings to the right, and at the left-hand bend fork right (straight on) and follow the byway northwards. With care, cross the A4130 again and take the surfaced path opposite, bearing left to a minor road. At the second entrance (**Highlands Farm**) on the right fork half-right

To visit St Agatha's Church, which dates from the mid 12th century, bear half-left at the war memorial.

over a stile and head diagonally up across two fields, crossing a stile. Cross another stile and continue up through the third field for 250m; to the right is the tree-crowned **Brightwell Barrow**. Bear left beside a water trough and head north-west down across the field and through the hedge gap. Turn right and follow the path round three sides of the field to the opposite side and head through the bushes to a gate on **Wittenham Clumps** (also known as the Sinodun Hills).

Tree-crowned Round Hill, one of the twin tops of the Wittenham Clumps (Sinodun Hills)

While the twin tops of the **Wittenham Clumps**, Round Hill and Castle Hill, are both crowned with beech copses, Castle Hill is also the site of the impressive earthworks of an Iron Age hill fort and was once home to the poem tree. In the mid 19th century Joseph Tubb of Warnborough Green carved a poem onto one of the beech trees; the tree has gone, but a memorial stone and plaque commemorate the poem. From the second top, Round Hill, there is a lovely panoramic view – to the west are the Berkshire Downs, to the north is the Oxfordshire plain and to the east are the Chiltern Hills.

To visit the Earth Trust centre (01865 407792) head west-south-west down from the second top, go through gates and cross the minor road; then retrace steps.

Either head west over **Castle Hill** (passing the poem tree memorial) or follow the earthworks clockwise to the opposite side and then head north-westwards to the second top (car park to left) and circle round to the view indicator. ◄ After admiring the view head north downhill, aiming for the church in **Little Wittenham**, go through a gate and continue along the left-hand field margin. Leave through a gate, turn right along the track past St Peter's Church and bear left downhill.

Inside the 14th-century **Church of St Peter** in Little Wittenham is a fine 17th-century memorial to Sir William Dunch, MP for Wallingford in the 1560s, and a figure of his wife, Mary Dunch, an aunt of Oliver Cromwell.

The route crosses the River Thame before following the River Thames

Soon cross two bridges, then cross a footbridge over the River Thames and go through a gate. Head diagonally left along the fenced bridleway. Go through a gate and continue along the fenced bridleway, which later curves right and follows the **Dyke Hills** for 300m.

The **Dyke Hills**, two parallel linear earthworks, were constructed as part of an Iron Age promontory settlement (protected on the other sides by the Thames and Thame). The earthworks were saved during the Victorian era by General Pitt Rivers, who helped initiate a national system to protect ancient monuments.

At the junction, with a path ahead, turn left along the fenced bridleway, continue past some houses and then along the surfaced track for 500m to the war memorial. Turn sharp right along the main street in **Dorchester on Thames**, passing a tea room and then The White Hart Hotel. Opposite The George Hotel a lane on the left leads to the impressive abbey church and museum.

DORCHESTER ON THAMES

The historic village of Dorchester on Thames, site of a former Roman settlement on the route between Alchester and Calleva Atrebatum (Silchester), has a history stretching back at least as far as the Iron Age. Jump forward several hundred years and it was here in AD635 that Cynegils, King of Wessex, was baptised by Birinus, a missionary sent by the Pope. This helped the spread of Christianity in England, and Dorchester on Thames became an important religious centre. Birinus built a Saxon cathedral church here; however, following the Norman Conquest, this was rebuilt as an Augustinian abbey.

Inside the Abbey Church of St Peter and St Paul there is a striking 14th-century Tree of Jesse window, a fine Norman lead font and some wonderful effigies. These include a 13th-century Crusader knight, and another commemorates John de Stonor (d.1354), Lord Chief Justice of England under Edward III, whose descendants live at Stonor House (Chilterns). Next door, in the former monastery guest house and grammar school, is a museum.

Continue along the main street past The Fleur de Lys Inn, and just after the octagonal toll house (left) fork right along Bridge End past the car park and toilets. Just after St Birinus Catholic Church turn right along Watling Lane and then immediately left along Wittenham Lane (track), signposted for the river and Wittenham. ▶ After the last house continue along the fenced path to the corner and bear left through the gate.

The 19th-century St Birinus Church was built by WW Wardell, who later emigrated to Australia and built Catholic cathedrals in Sydney and Melbourne.

The last part of the walk follows the Thames Path alongside the River Thames

The River Thame rises in the Vale of Aylesbury, whereas the 346km-long River Thames – England's longest river – starts out in Gloucestershire.

Continue past the end of the Dyke Hills (right), then past a pillbox (left), bear slightly left, go through a gate and continue south to the River Thames. Turn left (the walk now follows the Thames Path back to Shillingford), cross the footbridge over the River Thame, which joins the Thames here, and follow the riverside path for 1.3km. ◀ At the path junction (ahead is a cul-de-sac) turn left, go through a gate, carefully cross the **A4074** and turn right along the pavement to return to Shillingford.

WALK 5

Blewbury and the Astons

Start/finish	Car park at Blewbury village hall and shop (SU 530 860) along Westbrook Street, 500m north off the A417
Distance	13.7km (8½ miles)
Ascent	220m
Time	4hr
Map	OS Explorer 170
Refreshments	The Red Lion (01235 850403), The Blueberry (01235 850296) and Style Acre tea room at Savages Garden Centre (01235 850912) at Blewbury; The Chequers (01235 850800) at Aston Tirrold
Public transport	Bus service to Blewbury (A417) from Didcot rail station (excluding Sundays). (From the bus stop head west along the A417 and turn right along Nottingham Fee to the church and join the route here.)

This easy walk sets out from the picturesque village of Blewbury, with its historic church and wealth of thatched cottages, and passes the earthworks of a former Iron Age hill fort on Blewburton Hill before heading through the neighbouring villages of Aston Upthorpe and Aston Tirrold. The walk then heads south over the rolling Aston Upthorpe Downs before briefly meeting with the Ridgeway and then heading north past Churn Hill back down to Blewbury, with views including the Wittenham Clumps (Walk 4).

From the village hall at **Blewbury** head back to Westbrook Street and bear left along Church End to a junction. Fork right (straight on), shortly passing the churchyard (right). Continue along the enclosed path, cross the stream and then follow the track.

> **Blewbury**, once home to Kenneth Grahame, best known as the author of *The Wind in the Willows*, who lived for a while in a house in Westbrook Street (blue plaque), has many picturesque timber-framed and

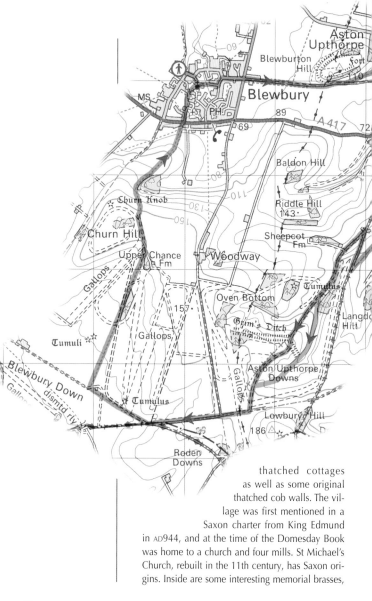

thatched cottages as well as some original thatched cob walls. The village was first mentioned in a Saxon charter from King Edmund in AD944, and at the time of the Domesday Book was home to a church and four mills. St Michael's Church, rebuilt in the 11th century, has Saxon origins. Inside are some interesting memorial brasses,

including one to Dame Alice Daunce (d.1523) and her husband Sir John, Surveyor-General to Henry VIII.

Turn left along South Street for 100m and then right along Bessels Lea to a junction. Cross the road (**B4016**) and keep ahead along the track past Winterbrook Farm, heading east gently up towards **Blewburton Hill**. ▸ A gate on the left at SU 544 859 gives access to the hill (open access land).

Keep ahead and go through the third gate on the left (SU 547 859), then follow the path diagonally across the field to the far-left corner. Descend some steps and follow the track as it curves left past houses to a junction beside Thorpe Farmhouse (left) and the All Saints Church (right) in **Aston Upthorpe**.

The hill is crowned with the remains of an Iron Age hill fort (400BC) and was later used as a Saxon cemetery (AD500).

The earthworks of the Iron Age hill fort on Blewburton Hill

The twin villages of **Aston Upthorpe** and **Aston Tirrold** are home to picturesque cottages, a pub and two interesting churches. All Saints Church in Aston Upthorpe is built on Saxon foundations and has an 11th-century nave and filled Norman doorway, while St Michael's Church, in Aston Tirrold, dates back to 1080.

Turn right along Thorpe Street, keep left at the junction, and at the next junction, beside the war memorial, go right along Baker Street in **Aston Tirrold**, with The Chequers pub on the left. Follow the lane as it swings right, and just before the first house on the left turn left along the enclosed path. Later keep ahead through the churchyard, passing St Michael's Church. Leave through a gate and turn right along the village street, ignoring Rectory Lane on the right. Keep left at the junction and head up to the **A417**.

St Michael's Church, in Aston Tirrold

With care, cross over and take the track opposite for 400m. Where the track curves left and starts to rise,

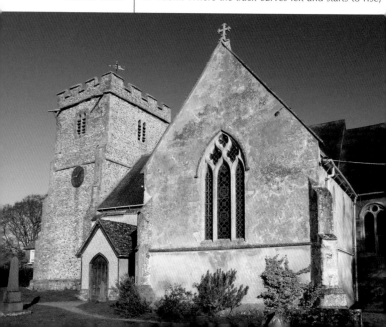

fork right and follow the bridleway, soon heading up past a small wood. Keep ahead alongside the left-hand hedge and then through a hedge gap to join a track. Turn sharp right down to a track junction with a barn opposite. Turn sharp left and follow the track for 200m to a junction with a house over to the right. Go straight on, with Langdon Wood (and **Langdon Hill**) on the left, to a three-way split at SU 544 836. Take the middle track (straight on) uphill (right is not a right of way) over **Aston Upthorpe Downs**; the left-hand track offers an alternative route via an area known as 'Juniper Valley' (open access land and an important site of special scientific interest).

Alternative route via 'Juniper Valley'

Fork left, go through the gate and follow the valley uphill. The species-rich chalk grassland contains the largest remaining stand of juniper scrub to be found in the Berkshire Downs (juniper berries are used to flavour gin). Later keep right along the valley and head up to a gate at SU 537 828; here rejoin the main walk by turning left (adds 200m).

Continue uphill, passing a small copse beside the remains of **Grim's Ditch**, later passing a gate on the left. ▸ Continue up to a track junction, turn right, ignore a crossing route and later join the Ridgeway. Continue westwards downhill for 100m and fork right heading west-north-west (Ridgeway goes straight on) for 700m, later passing just left of some trees and scrub and a farm building to reach a concrete track.

The alternative route rejoins here.

Turn right (north-north-east) following a path between open fields. After 750m follow the edge of a wood on the right and keep ahead up to a track beside a small wood near **Upper Chance Farm** to the right. Bear left, soon passing to the right of **Churn Hill**. Where the track curves left, fork right and follow the path downhill. ▸ Continue downhill to a marker where the path splits into two parallel routes heading down to Blewbury. Take the right-hand path, which is drier and offers some views of Blewburton Hill and the distant Chiltern Hills.

A gate on the right in the trees leads to the open access land of Lid's Bottom.

The Red Lion in Blewbury, passed at the end of the walk

Continue down the track, to the A417 in Blewbury (275m to the right is The Blueberry pub and bus stop; 400m to the left is the farm shop and café). Cross straight over and follow Nottingham Fee. Keep right (straight on) at the split beside a thatched cottage to reach The Red Lion where the road curves right. Go straight on between thatched walls, cross a footbridge and follow the right-hand edge of an open grassy area. Continue along the enclosed path and soon pass just left of St Michael's Church. Leave through a gate and turn left, retracing the outward route back to the village hall.

Heading north down towards the Letcombe villages on Walk 10

WALK 6
West Ilsley and Farnborough

Start/finish	Junction of Main Street and Bury Lane beside the church in West Ilsley (SU 473 825); roadside parking nearby. Alternative parking/start: car park on East Hendred Down (SU 458 850) or junction of the Ridgeway and B4494 (SU 418 841)
Distance	14.7km (9 miles)
Ascent	215m
Time	4hr
Map	OS Explorer 170
Refreshments	The Harrow at West Ilsley (01635 281260)
Public transport	Limited bus service to West Ilsley (Main Street) from Newbury (excluding Sundays)

Setting out from West Ilsley, the walk heads west across open farmland to reach the peaceful village of Farnborough, once home to Sir John Betjeman. It then follows the Ridgeway along the crest of the downs, with views out over the Oxfordshire plain, and passes two monuments before following gallops back down to West Ilsley.

The picturesque village of **West Ilsley** was the original home of the Morland Brewery. John Morland, a local farmer, started brewing his much-sought-after ale here in 1711; the business moved to Abingdon in 1887 and was bought by Greene King in 2000. The village's All Saints Church underwent major alterations in the 1870s, although the underlying fabric of the church is much older. Inside there is a fine carved-wood Jacobean pulpit, rood screen and cross.

Stand facing All Saints Church and turn right (west) along Main Street, later passing the duck pond and Millennium gazebo (left), Catmore Road junction and The Harrow

The Harrow, West Ilsley

pub (right) overlooking the cricket pitch. From the pub continue up along the main road for 500m and turn left through a field entrance. Immediately turn right and continue westwards, following the hedge on the right to a track. Turn left and follow the track south-westwards, continue past the buildings at **Starveall Farm** and start rising up **Old Down**.

Near the top of the rise enter a field and keep ahead, following the fence on the right to join a crossing restricted byway (Old Street). Take a moment to admire the views. Turn left for 75m, then turn right through a gap in the bushes. Head west across the field, and continue through the next field following the right-hand margin at first. Keep straight on past the water tower to a road in **Farnborough** and bear left; shortly look right for a view of the mid 18th-century Old Rectory.

The poet laureate **Sir John Betjeman** (1906–1984) lived at the Old Rectory in Farnborough for several years (the garden is occasionally open through the National Gardens Scheme). Step inside All Saints Church to see a lovely stained-glass memorial window to Betjeman designed by John Piper.

49

Colourful window commemorating Sir John Betjeman, All Saints Church, Farnborough

Where the road curves right, go straight on to enter the churchyard, passing just left of All Saints Church. Keep ahead, leave the churchyard and continue through the field, passing to the left of a trig point and bungalow before bearing right and leaving through a gate. Go down the steps, turn left (west) along the road and keep ahead at the junction.

Just before the speed sign at the edge of the village turn right onto a track (byway) and keep left to follow the tree-shaded route for 1.4km. Go through a gate and continue diagonally across the field, passing a wooden electricity pole; to the right is

Lockinge Kiln Farm and a communications mast. Go through a gate a short way to the left of the field corner, cross the road (**B4494**) and continue in the same direction (if overgrown, turn right for 20m then left through the gates), soon following a track through trees.

At the end of the trees turn sharp right, keeping the trees on the right and open field to the left. Cross back over the road and continue, still with trees on the right, to join the Ridgeway and turn right; the walk now follows the Ridgeway for 4.4km. ▶ Follow the Ridgeway eastwards, passing a **monument** after 350m.

A short way to the left is a car park at SU 418 841 that can be used as an alternative parking/start point.

The monument is to **Colonel Robert Loyd-Lindsay** (1832–1901), later Lord Wantage of Lockinge, a founding member of the British Red Cross and a noted soldier during the Crimean War, who was

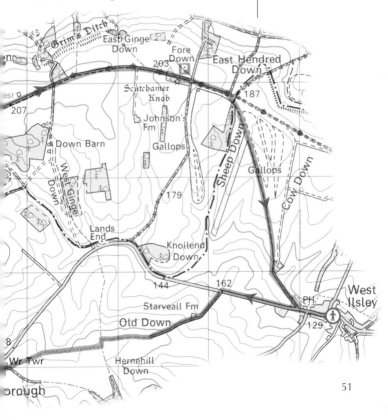

awarded the Victoria Cross. He was responsible for the statue of King Alfred in Wantage and the building of East Lockinge in the 1860s; he is buried at Holy Trinity Church in Ardington (Walk 7).

Head north-east slightly downhill to some fir trees and keep along the wide grassy track, passing a **reservoir** (hidden by trees). At a crossing bridleway (SU 442 849), just before a copse, through the gate on the left is a sarsen stone and memorial plaque to Lady Penelope Betjeman (1910–1986). Continue along the Ridgeway to pass a trig point on Cuckhamsley Hill (203m). The gate on the right gives access to the unusual earthwork of **Scutchamer Knob** – as for what it was, nobody really knows, although legend has it as the burial site of the Saxon King Cwichelm.

Keep ahead at the crossing tarmac track, passing a parking area (SU 458 850 – an alternative parking/start point), and continue along the Ridgeway for 450m admiring the views. To the north-east and near is the Harwell complex; further away are the twin tops of the Wittenham Clumps (Walk 4), and some 25km away is the Chiltern scarp.

Harwell, now the Harwell Science and Innovation Campus, was established in 1946 on the site of a former Second World War airfield as Britain's first Atomic Energy Research Establishment, including the first nuclear reactor in Western Europe (GLEEP – the Graphite Low Energy Experimental Pile). The site is now home to the Rutherford Appleton Laboratory and includes the ISIS neutron source and the Diamond Light Source Synchrotron (the large metal disc-shaped building).

At a crossing bridleway (SU 462 848), turn right across the gallop and then left to follow the fence on your right heading south-south-east for 1.8km. Keep ahead down the track towards West Ilsley and then bear left (straight on) along the main road, passing The Harrow pub back to the start.

WALK 7
Ardington and the Hendreds

Start/finish	Village shop on the High Street in Ardington, 500m south off A417 (SU 431 884); on-street parking in village
Distance	9.5km (6 miles)
Ascent	110m
Time	2½hr
Map	OS Explorer 170
Refreshments	The Boars Head (01235 835466) and village shop/tea room (01235 833237) at Ardington; The Wheatsheaf (01235 833229), The Eyston Arms (01235 833320) and shop at East Hendred
Public transport	Daily bus services to Ardington and East Hendred from Oxford, Didcot and Wantage

Situated along the northern edge of the downs are a number of picturesque villages with thatched cottages and historic churches. This easy half-day walk weaves its way through three of these villages – Ardington and the twin villages of West and East Hendred – passing three pubs, a tea room and historic Ardington House on the way.

Face the village shop and tea room in **Ardington** and turn right along the High Street for 20m. Turn right along Church Street for 75m and go left through a brick archway. Follow the enclosed path as it swings right and left to reach a surfaced track beside some houses. Turn right to a junction and then go left, following the surfaced track to some barns (left) at **Red Barn**.

Continue along the wide grassy path between fields, cross **Ginge Brook** via a footbridge, then a stile, and go through the churchyard at **West Hendred**. ▶ Leave through the lychgate and head up to a T-junction, then turn left along the village street for 125m. At the slight left bend go right along the driveway, and immediately after the house turn left along the enclosed surfaced

The 14th-century Holy Trinity Church houses a carved-wood Jacobean pulpit and some medieval glass.

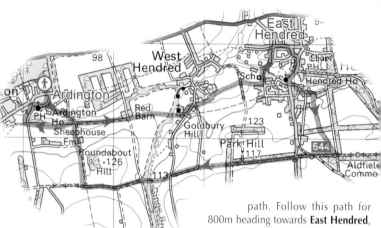

path. Follow this path for 800m heading towards **East Hendred**, ignoring a crossing track. Turn left down the lane (school on left) for 150m, and then fork right down to a stream and houses (right). Keep ahead up Fordy Lane and then left (straight on) along Cat Street to a four-way junction.

Turn right along Orchard Lane for 200m, and then turn right at the junction (Chapel Square). Keep left at the next junction to pass The Wheatsheaf (left) and continue to a junction beside Champs Chapel (museum).

The village shop at East Hendred

EAST HENDRED

East Hendred, the larger of the two Hendred villages, has a wealth of 16th- and 17th-century brick and timber-framed houses, including a fine example of Tudor brickwork at the village shop. Hendred House, based round a 15th-century hall house, was passed to the Eystons through marriage in the 15th century and it has been their family home ever since. The family are related by marriage to Sir Thomas More, one-time Chancellor to Henry VIII, who was executed along with John Fisher, Bishop of Rochester, in 1535.

The Church of St Augustine of Canterbury has an interesting, but hidden, faceless clock. Built in 1525 by John Seymour of Wantage it is one of the oldest clocks in England, and still chimes the hours and quarters as it has for almost 500 years, while every three hours it plays the 'Angel's song' by Orlando Gibbons. The small but interesting Champs Chapel Museum is housed in the former 15th-century Chapel of Jesus of Bethlehem built by Carthusian monks from Sheen, Surrey (open Sunday afternoons during the summer).

Turn right (south) along the High Street, passing The Eyston Arms, village shop and then the tree-lined drive that leads to Hendred House. At the cross-junction beside the Church of St Augustine of Canterbury (right), turn left along St Mary's Road, and after curving right turn left beside St

The Church of St Augustine of Canterbury

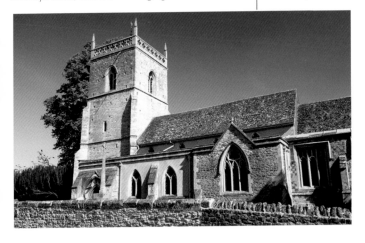

The Victorian-Gothic Roman Catholic church was built by the Eyston family in the 1860s and contains some good stained-glass windows.

Mary's Church. ◄ Where the lane curves right fork left along the gravel drive past Cozens Farm; keep ahead along the restricted byway as it curves right to a junction.

Take the right-hand fork (southwards) along the enclosed route for 700m, ignoring a crossing track, to reach a cross-track junction beside stands of trees at **Aldfield Common**. Turn right (west) and follow the track (trees on left), and then at the junction keep ahead along the surfaced track. Cross the minor road and continue along the track (trees on right). After passing through a belt of trees keep ahead between fields. Cross another minor road and follow the left-hand field boundary, later dropping down to cross **Ginge Brook** via a footbridge in the trees. Keep straight on for 650m to a crossing bridleway and turn right (northwards) gently downhill, keeping **Roundabout Hill** on the right. Keep ahead past the barn at **Sheephouse Farm** to arrive at the cross-junction passed earlier.

Picturesque Ardington House

Turn left along the grassy path with trees on the right; soon there is a great view of Ardington House to the right.

> Overlooking a small lake is the beautifully symmetrical grey and red-brick Baroque **Ardington House**. The house, built for Edward Clarke in 1720 and once owned by Lord Wantage (who is buried at the local church), has been the Baring family home for several generations. Hidden within the house is a stunning imperial staircase, with two matching flights leading into one, and a wood-panelled dining room that the former poet laureate Sir John Betjeman described as 'the nicest dining room in Oxfordshire' (opening times, 01235 821566).

Keep ahead and then turn right along the minor road towards Ardington, crossing Ardington Brook to a junction. Turn right along Church Street, passing Holy Trinity Church.

> **Holy Trinity Church** has a fine Norman doorway and a 14th-century preaching cross. Inside is a marble figure by Edward Bailey, who designed Nelson's Column in Trafalgar Square, London.

Continue past The Boars Head pub, then the entrance to Ardington House, following the road as it curves left to a T-junction. Turn left back to the start.

WALK 8

Great Shefford, Chaddleworth and East Garston

Start/finish	Junction of Church Street and A338 in Great Shefford opposite The Swan Inn (SU 383 752); limited on-street parking along Church Street
Distance	14.4km (9 miles)
Ascent	290m
Time	4hr
Map	OS Explorer 158
Refreshments	The Great Shefford (01488 648462) and shop at Great Shefford; The Queens Arms (01488 648757) at East Garston
Public transport	Bus services to Great Shefford from Newbury and Lambourn (excluding Sundays)

The first part of the walk follows the Lambourn Valley Way between Great Shefford and its smaller neighbour, East Shefford; the shared name is probably derived from 'sheep ford'. After a short detour to visit East Shefford's historic church the walk passes through Chaddleworth before following an undulating route past the horse-racing stables at Whatcombe to reach East Garston. The final leg meanders alongside the River Lambourn back to Great Shefford.

At the junction of Church Street and the A338 in **Great Shefford**, with The Great Shefford pub opposite, turn left and cross the footbridge. Follow the enclosed path and then turn right along Station Road to rejoin the A338. Turn left, and just after the service station (right) turn right across the road to a track; the walk is now following the Lambourn Valley Way. Follow the track towards East Shefford for 500m to a cross-track junction (SU 390 749), where the main route goes left. At the junction there is the option to take a short detour to the Church of St Thomas (300m each way).

To visit the church, turn right down the track to a track junction just before the bridge over the River

Lambourn and turn left, passing **East Shefford House** (left), then turn left through a gate to the church (key in box by the gate). Retrace your steps to the cross-track junction and go straight ahead.

Step inside the church to see the tomb of Sir Thomas Fettiplace and his wife, Lady Beatrice

> The little Norman **Church of St Thomas** at East Shefford, cared for by the Churches Conservation Trust, is well worth a visit. Step inside to see fragments of medieval wall paintings and several memorials to the Fettiplaces, who once held the manor. These include the tomb, with recumbent effigies, of Sir Thomas Fettiplace (d.1442) and his wife, Lady Beatrice (d.1447), and an early 16th-century canopied tomb, with brass inlays, of John and Dorothy Fettiplace.

On the main route, head north-east along the fenced permissive path with the farm buildings to the right and follow the path as it turns right. Turn left up the track (bridleway) for 800m to a crossing path and turn right over the stile. Head north-eastwards across the field and through a gap in the high hedge. The path now crosses a golf course – take care. Follow the marker posts across the fairways

and through
belts of trees before leaving the golf course and entering
a field. Pass just right of a stand of trees, aiming for the
right-hand field boundary beside a marker post. Turn right

through the bushes, re-entering the golf course, and turn left following the left-hand margin.

At the marker post bear half-right across the grass and continue through the planta-tion, keeping to the path as it turns right and left. Cross the minor road and fol-low the path opposite for 900m through the field, keeping the line of trees on the right. Dogleg into the right-hand field and follow the left-hand boundary to a cross-junction at the field corner. Turn left and then imme-diately right along the enclosed path (garden on right). Follow the gravel track to a minor road in **Chaddleworth** and turn left.

Follow the street north-west-wards keeping ahead at the first junction, then at the next junction (Botmoor Way) turn right and follow the high brick wall to its end. Continue through the churchyard, passing just left of St Andrew's Church, and leave through a gate. Turn left and shortly enter a field via a gate.

The manor at **Chaddleworth** was given to Robert d'Oyley by William the Conqueror and later belonged to the mother of Edward I. In the 16th cen-tury Henry VIII exchanged Chaddleworth for land in London, including St James' Park, while Westminster got the parish of Chaddleworth; the Dean and Chapter of Westminster are still Chaddleworth's patrons. The 12th-century St Andrew's Church (with later additions) has the remains of a medi-eval preaching cross, a fine Norman zig-zag carved doorway and two 17th-century side chapels belonging to the Blandy and Wroughton families.

Head diagonally right down across the field to the lower-right corner. Cross the stile and follow the minor road downhill for 150m before forking left down a track. At the bottom, cross the minor road and take the track opposite, passing to the left of **Manor Farm**. Cross a stile and continue up the left-hand field boundary over the hill. At the hedge, turn left and right over stiles and continue down through two fields.

Cross the **A338** and follow the minor road opposite (signposted to Whatcombe and South Fawley) for 125m. Turn left through the gated entrance to **Whatcombe** and follow the gravel track (bridleway) running parallel with the hedge and driveway.

The **training stables** at Whatcombe, built on the site of a former medieval village that was mentioned in the Domesday Book, have produced several famous racehorses including Snurge (spot the life-size bronze statue).

After 400m keep ahead along the driveway, passing to the left of buildings, and immediately fork left along a track heading uphill. Near the top, where the track curves left, go straight on across the grassy area, later passing a gate and some trees. Bear slightly left across the field corner on **Kite Hill**.

Go through a gap in the hedge, ignore the crossing route and follow the bridleway straight on down across the field, later rising to a fingerpost. Continue across the next field in the same direction for 900m to a cross-junction on the far side. Stay in the field and turn left following the byway along the field boundary as it skirts clockwise round the trees of Furze Border (note the right of way on the map goes through the trees). Keep ahead along the track for 1.1km, passing a trig point, and start descending to a track junction. Turn right (north-west) along the track. ◀

For a slightly shorter walk (by 1.5km/ 1 mile), missing out East Garston, continue downhill past Maidencourt Farm to rejoin the main walk beside the River Lambourn.

Heading down through fields on the way to Whatcombe

The River Lambourn at Maidencourt Farm

The short-cut rejoins the main route here.

Follow the track for 800m to a minor road at **East Garston**. Turn left and pass the abutments of a disused railway bridge (this was the Lambourn Valley Railway, which opened in 1898 and ran between Lambourn and Newbury). Bear left at the junction for 300m, passing some thatched cottages overlooking the River Lambourn (a byway on the right leads to The Queens Arms pub). Where the lane bears right go straight on along the track. Continue alongside the River Lambourn to **Maidencourt Farm** and turn right along the driveway over the bridge. ◄

After 125m turn left through a gate and follow the path across the field to a gate just left of the house. Continue along the fenced path and then keep ahead through two fields, heading towards Great Shefford and passing to the left of St Mary's Church.

The 12th-century **St Mary's Church** has a rare round tower, one of only two in Berkshire (the other being at St Gregory's Church at Welford; most are located in East Anglia), a carved Norman font and the remains of an old preaching cross in the churchyard.

Go through a gate and turn right along the track as it curves left. Follow the main road back to the start.

WALK 9
Lambourn and Eastbury

Start/finish	Market Place, Lambourn (SU 326 789); car park off the High Street behind the library
Distance	11.2km (7 miles)
Ascent	265m
Time	3¼hr
Map	OS Explorer 158
Refreshments	The George (01488 674133), Goodies Café (01488 208470) and shops at Lambourn; The Plough (01488 71312) at Eastbury
Public transport	Bus services to Lambourn from Newbury (excluding Sundays)

From Lambourn the walk heads south before meandering across fields and through woods to arrive at picturesque Eastbury, complete with thatched cottages, a pub and a church with a lovely engraved window. The return route follows tracks and paths to pass a small nature reserve before heading downhill with a view over the Lambourn Valley (known as the 'Valley of the Racehorse' due to the number of horse-training stables in the area) to arrive back in Lambourn.

Picturesque **Lambourn**, said to have been the model for Maryland in Thomas Hardy's novel *Jude the Obscure*, is centred around St Michael and All Angels Church and the adjoining Market Place, complete with its old stone market cross from the reign of Henry VI. Parts of the church, which is based on a typical cruciform design with a central tower, date back to Norman times. Inside there are several notable monuments, including the impressive alabaster tomb of Sir Thomas Essex of Lambourn Place (d.1558) and his wife, Margaret. Behind the church is the red-brick castellated entrance to the Isbury Almshouses, originally built by John Estbury in 1502.

From the crossroads beside the Market Place head south-west along the High Street with The George pub on the left, passing the car park entrance on the right (from where you can start the walk) and then Goodies Café (right). Immediately after the junction with Edwards Hill road on the left, fork half-left up the track past houses to a lane and bear right uphill past a school. At the split take the right-hand lane (bridleway sign) to its end. Continue along the bridleway over **Coppington Hill**, and follow the left-hand field margin down to a track near **Boldstart Farm**. Keep ahead along the track, heading uphill, and where this turns right go straight on and follow the concrete track towards **Willis Farm**.

Keep left of a barn, and where the track turns right to the house go left through a gate. Head up through the field, passing the power-line to a path junction at the top-left corner. Turn left, soon passing the thatched Dances Cottage (left), and then turn right along the track. Keep ahead at the junction by some trees to reach a crossing path and turn left down across the field. Keep ahead down through Ox Wood to a track and turn left down to a track junction.

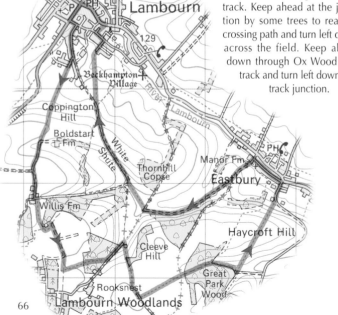

Turn sharp right following the track up **Cleeve Hill** (Cleeve Cottage on the left) for 550m to reach a crossing path. Turn left, following the grassy strip and then continuing across the field. Go through a hedge gap, cross over the track and continue across the narrow field. Keep ahead down through **Great Park Wood**, ignore a path to the left and soon enter a field. Follow the trees on the right to a cross-path junction beside the hedge and turn left (north-north-east) up **Haycroft Hill** (across the open field) before heading down towards **Eastbury**, admiring the views on the way. Pass to the right of a barn, continue down the minor road to a junction and take the first turning on the left.

Follow the lane, with the River Lambourn on the right, past thatched cottages and the Church of St James the Greater (left). At the junction turn left (Corney Street); just to the right across the bridge is The Plough.

Picturesque **Eastbury** has a lovely collection of 16th- and 17th-century cottages overlooking the River Lambourn. Inside the Church of St James

Heading down towards Eastbury from Haycroft Hill

The River Lambourn at Eastbury

the Greater is a stunning engraved window by Sir Laurence Whistler (a leading exponent of hand engraving during the 20th century), a fitting tribute to the poet Edward Thomas (1878–1917) and his wife, Helen. After Thomas was killed in action at the Battle of Arras during the First World War, his widow moved to Eastbury.

Head up Corney Street (track), following the main track (ignoring a path to the left) to a split (fingerpost) and fork left, keeping the trees on the left and following the stony track (byway) uphill to a fingerpost. Fork right along the bridleway (grassy track) and then keep ahead alongside Cleeve Wood (left), with an open field on the right. Go straight over the crossing track, through a gate and keep ahead across the corner of the field before leaving through another gate. Bear right (north-west) up the track – **White Shute**. After 150m a gate on the right gives access to Watts Bank nature reserve.

Watts Bank is a small chalk grassland nature reserve cared for by the Berks, Bucks and Oxon Wildlife Trust (BBOWT). Over 30 species of butterfly have been recorded here as well as plants including orchids (spotted, southern marsh and fragrant), harebells and autumn gentians.

Follow the track over the brow of the hill, start heading downhill and fork half-right on a path heading north down across the field towards **Lambourn** (not the path following the right-hand hedge). Pass through the hedge and continue along the enclosed path towards the houses. Go through a gate, down some steps and follow the estate road (Coppington Gardens) to a T-junction. Turn left for 75m and then right along Blind Lane to a path junction. Turn left and follow the enclosed path to a road beside Bodman Close. Bear left along the street (Newbury Street) back to the Market Place; for the car park turn left at the crossroads following the High Street for 120m to the car park on the right.

WALK 10
The Ridgeway and the Letcombe villages

Start/finish	Sparsholt Firs car park at the junction of the Ridgeway and B4001 (SU 343 850)
Distance	12.5km (7¾ miles)
Ascent	225m
Time	3½hr
Map	OS Explorer 170
Refreshments	Café/shop and The Greyhound Inn (01235 771969) at Letcombe Regis
Public transport	Buses from Wantage stop at Letcombe Regis and Letcombe Bassett (excluding Sundays)

The walk heads east along the Ridgeway, looking out across the convoluted contours of Crowhole Bottom and the Devil's Punchbowl before dropping down to meander through the picturesque neighbouring villages of Letcombe Regis and Letcombe Bassett. Running between the villages is the Letcombe Brook, once noted for its watercress. The return route climbs back up to the Ridgeway and retraces the outward route, offering different views.

Head eastwards along the Ridgeway. Soon a path on the left offers an optional detour to the convoluted contours of Devil's Punchbowl and Crowhole Bottom. ◀ Continue on the Ridgeway for 3.8km, with views to the north across the Vale of White Horse and Oxfordshire, keeping ahead at **Gramp's Hill** road and then **Smith's Hill**. On reaching a footpath sign, just after passing a seat, turn left over the stile.

This extensive area of unimproved chalk grassland (open access land) is home to a number of plants including gentians and orchids.

Just off route, over to the right are the earthworks of Segsbury (or Letcombe) Castle, a former Iron Age hill fort. To visit, continue eastwards along the Ridgeway for 500m to Segsbury Farm and turn left along the track

The earthworks of Segsbury Castle, a former Iron Age hill fort, lie near the route

for 100m; a stile on the right gives permissive access (please observe any changes).

Continuing on the main route, from the stile head north down across the field, cross a stile at the trees and keep ahead steeply downhill, following the right-hand

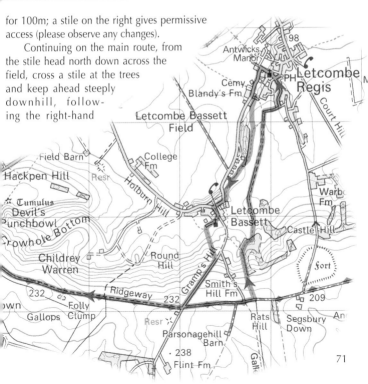

boundary and crossing another stile. At the bottom go uphill slightly, and a few metres before the field corner turn right over a stile. Follow the path through the trees, cross a stile and keep ahead through the field. Leave via a stile in the north corner and turn left along the bridleway, later passing through a gate.

Continue through another gate to a junction and keep ahead, soon following the enclosed track as it swings right to a road in **Letcombe Regis**. Turn left and follow the road (South Street) down through the village to a four-way junction beside St Andrew's Church; 100m to the right (Main Street) is The Greyhound pub on the right.

The name **Letcombe** comes from 'Ledecumbe', meaning 'the brook (lede) in the valley'; the 'Regis' part was added during the reign of Richard II. 'Bassett', in the name of the neighbouring village of Letcombe Bassett, is from the Norman baron Richard Bassett, who was lord of the manor in the mid 12th century. The 12th-century St Andrew's Church has the remains of a medieval cross just inside the gate.

Turn left, keeping the church on the right, and fork right at the thatch-roofed village shop and café. After passing Castle Gardens on the right, turn right along the enclosed path. Cross a footbridge and keep ahead to a lane. Turn left along the lane and pass the recreation ground and car park and then the **cemetery**, both on the right. Once level with the entrance to **Blandy's Farm**, turn left along the track past some cottages.

Cross the footbridge, go through a gate and bear right along the gravel path. Pass a gate and information board and follow the path ahead through the Letcombe Valley Nature Reserve before bearing left up steps to leave through a gate. Cared for by the Berks, Bucks and Oxon Wildlife Trust (BBOWT), the nature reserve is centred on the chalk stream habitat of the Letcombe Brook, which is home to water voles, kingfishers and dragonflies.

Turn right along the enclosed path to join a road with Rectory Lane off to the left. Follow the minor road south-westwards through **Letcombe Bassett** to a junction with a small triangular green and seat.

Letcombe Bassett and the Letcombe Brook were, at one time, noted for their watercress, and 'Bassett cress' was once a familiar cry in London's Covent Garden market. The Wessex author Thomas Hardy referred to the village as 'Cresscombe' in his novel *Jude the Obscure* (100m along the lane to the west of the small green is a thatched cottage said to have been the inspiration for Arabella's cottage in the novel). The 13th-century St Michael's and All Angels Church retains some fine examples of Norman orna-mentation. To the left of the entrance is a blocked-up doorway, and still discernible are the four signs of the Evangelists – the eagle of St John, the lion of St Mark, the angel of St Matthew and the ox of St Luke.

Turn left uphill (Gramp's Hill) to a split at a thatched cottage and fork right along Forsters Lane to pass the Church of St Michael and All Angels. At the end of the lane go through a gate and bear half-left in the field, keeping right of a line of trees to a gate and continue uphill with views to the right. At the top bear right for 15m, then left through the trees to join a lane – Gramp's Hill. Turn right up the lane to rejoin the Ridgeway and turn right, retracing the outward route for 3km back to the start.

WALK 11

*Compton Beauchamp, Woolstone
and the Uffington White Horse*

Start/finish	National Trust Whitehorse Hill car park (pay and display), just south of Woolstone off the B4507 (SU 292 865)
Distance	11.9km (7½ miles)
Ascent	225m
Time	3½hr
Map	OS Explorer 170
Refreshments	The White Horse (01367 820726) at Woolstone; Tea Pot tea room at Britchcombe Farm on summer weekends (01367 821022)
Public transport	Saturday bus service between Swindon and Wantage stops at SU 294 871; daily buses (excluding Sundays) between Swindon and Newbury stop at Ashbury Folly on B4000 (SU 273 843, 1km off route)

The first part of the walk heads west along the Ridgeway to visit Wayland's Smithy (long barrow) before heading down to the vale and meandering through Compton Beauchamp and Woolstone. A stiff climb at Britchcombe Farm leads back to the Ridgeway and Whitehorse Hill, described by Thomas Hughes, author of *Tom Brown's Schooldays*, as 'a place that you won't ever forget' – and it really is a special place. Take time to ponder why the 3000-year-old stylised galloping figure of the Uffington White Horse was made and enjoy the view across the Vale of White Horse.

From the car park turn left up the access road, and where this swings left keep ahead to a cross-track junction. Turn right along the Ridgeway; after 1.5km take a short detour through the gate on the right to visit **Wayland's Smithy**.

Wayland's Smithy, a Neolithic long barrow surrounded by trees, dates from 3700BC. The barrow, which is named after Wayland, a magical smith in

Norse mythology, was first mentioned in AD955. Wayland was said to own a white horse, and the close proximity of the Uffington White Horse may explain the naming of this barrow. A local legend states that any traveller whose horse required a shoe should leave it with a coin next to the tomb. On returning the horse would be shod and the coin gone; Sir Walter Scott referred to the legend in his novel *Kenilworth*.

Wayland's Smithy – a Neolithic long barrow just off the Ridgeway

Continue on the Ridgeway a short distance, and at the next cross-junction turn right, now following the D'Arcy Dalton Way.

The 107km (66 mile) **D'Arcy Dalton Way** runs north–south between Wormleighton in Warwickshire and Wayland's Smithy, linking with the Oxford Canal path, the Oxfordshire Way, the Thames Path and the Ridgeway.

Pass some trees and continue down **Odstone Hill** (concrete track) to a road (**B4507**). Cross diagonally left and continue down the surfaced drive towards **Odstone Farm**. Where the drive goes left, keep ahead to the track end beside a house on the right. Continue straight on, go through a gate and turn right to quickly cross a stile beside the gate.

Follow the right-hand edge through three fields, crossing a stile and footbridge at the first corner. At the corner of the third field, pass through the trees and head east-north-east across a fourth field (track). Continue in a similar direction aiming for the picturesque St Swithun's Church in **Compton Beauchamp**, later following the

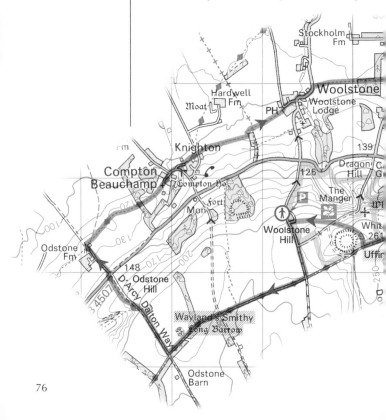

fence on the right with the church to the right. Go through a gate and bear left along the surfaced track; to visit the church turn right.

> Go inside the 13th-century St Swithun's Church in **Compton Beauchamp** to see the wall paintings by Lydia Lawrence, daughter of Sir James Bacon (1798–1895), Vice-Chancellor from 1870 to 1886, who lived at Compton Beauchamp House. The present house dates from around 1600, and replaced an earlier building that was once the home of the King's Councillor Sir Thomas Fettiplace.

Follow the drive to the minor road and go straight on (look back for a glimpse of Compton House). As the road curves right and rises, go through a gate and continue across the field, aiming just left of a small cottage. Cross the stile and continue beside trees, cross another stile and follow the right-hand field edge. Keep ahead over the minor road near **Knighton** (right), cross a stile and follow the right-hand field margin for 125m (the D'Arcy Dalton Way forks left). Cross a stile and continue beside a line of trees and then follow the fence line through another field; at the field corner go left for 50m and then turn right. Cross a stile and footbridge and go through the bushes to a byway (Hardwell Lane).

Go left for a few metres and then right, cross the stile and follow the right-hand margin through three fields. Keep ahead along the track and then straight on along the lane through the picturesque spring-line village of **Woolstone**, passing the 16th-century White Horse pub.

Keep left at the junction, and where the road turns hard left go straight on through a gate, following the right-hand margin through two fields. Keep ahead through trees and follow the hedge on the left to leave through a gate.

Turn right along the minor road for 25m and then left through a gate. Follow the right-hand margin, with trees to the left, to a path junction with a footbridge and open field ahead. Do not cross the footbridge but turn right, following the path through the trees before bearing left over a footbridge and entering a different field.

Turn right along the right-hand margin, cross a footbridge at the corner and keep ahead through the next field for 60m before turning right through two gates to enter a field. Turn left, following the left-hand fence, cross a stile and keep ahead past the campsite to a road with **Britchcombe Farm** opposite (summer weekend tea room). Cross the road and turn left for 60m to the driveway on the right. Fork slightly right here up the waymarked path (steps). Go through the gate and turn right through another gate. Keep ahead steeply uphill through fields separated by gates – take a breather on the way up and admire the views – before joining the Ridgeway.

Turn right along the track for 750m and then right through a gate at the fingerpost. Head across the field to the trig point beside the earthworks of the Iron Age hill fort on **Whitehorse Hill**; this is the highest point in Oxfordshire at 261m.

From Whitehorse Hill there is a great **view** – to the north is the open expanse of the Vale of White Horse; east-north-east are the Chiltern Hills way in the distance (on a clear day, and with binoculars, the Stokenchurch transmitter is just visible, 45km away); south-east are the rolling contours of the Lambourn Downs; south-west is Liddington Castle, with Barbury Castle (Walk 16) further on and slightly to the right (look for the stands of trees).

Head north for 150m to reach the **white-horse hill figure**, with Dragon Hill further downhill (the best view of the horse is from the air).

The magical outline of the Uffington White Horse

THE UFFINGTON WHITE HORSE

This white horse is the oldest in the country, and although it was first mentioned in a medieval manuscript from Abingdon Abbey, recent excavations and new dating techniques have shown that the horse was carved around 3000 years ago in the Bronze Age. It was GK Chesterton (1874–1936), in his 'Ballad of the White Horse' (1911), who summed up the age of the horse perfectly:

> Before the gods that made the gods
> Had seen their sunrise pass,
> The White Horse of the White Horse Vale
> Was cut out of the grass.

We may know the age of the carving with some degree of accuracy, but as to its purpose, we'll probably never really know.

The figure's remarkable state of preservation has been put down to the 'scouring fairs', where local people would gather to help clean it. Thomas Hughes (1822–1896), who spent his childhood in the village of Uffington, wrote about the area in *Tom Brown's Schooldays* (1856), and also about the scouring rituals in *The Scouring of the White Horse* (1859). (The small museum in nearby Uffington (01367 820259), Hughes' birthplace, is worth a visit for those interested in his life and work.)

The small, flat-topped mound of Dragon Hill, beneath the White Horse, is where St George is reputed to have killed the dragon. The steep-sided coombe, or dry valley, to the left (west) of Dragon Hill is known as The Manger, and legend has it that the White Horse goes there to feed.

After admiring the view bear left (west) along a defined path and descend to cross a minor road. Go through the gate and continue westwards back to the car park in the trees.

WALK 12
Ashbury and Bishopstone

Start/finish	Ashbury Folly car park (SU 273 843), just south-east of Ashbury where the Ridgeway crosses the B4000
Distance	10.4km (6½ miles)
Ascent	165m
Time	3hr
Map	OS Explorer 170
Refreshments	The Rose and Crown Inn (01793 378354) and village shop and tea room (01793 710068) at Ashbury; The Royal Oak (01793 790481) at Bishopstone
Public transport	Buses between Swindon and Newbury stop at Ashbury Folly (excluding Sundays)

The first part of this walk follows the Ridgeway before heading downhill to explore two picturesque spring-line villages – Ashbury and Bishopstone – tucked below the downs. The route then heads back up to the Ridgeway to make its return. The walk also passes through two interesting coombes, or dry valleys, with distant views.

Heading down through Kingstone Coombes towards Ashbury

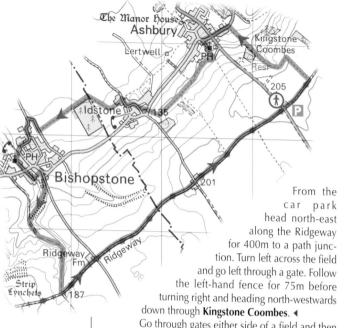

From the car park head north-east along the Ridgeway for 400m to a path junction. Turn left across the field and go left through a gate. Follow the left-hand fence for 75m before turning right and heading north-westwards down through **Kingstone Coombes**. ◀

These dry valleys were formed when most of Britain was buried beneath a layer of ice.

Go through gates either side of a field and then follow the enclosed track to a road (**B4507**) at **Ashbury**. Turn left, soon passing the village shop and tea room, keep ahead at the crossroads (**B4000**) and immediately after The Rose and Crown Inn turn left up Church Lane; to the right is the village green and war memorial.

The picturesque village of **Ashbury** – mentioned in Saxon times as 'Aescaesbyries' ('camp of the ash trees') – with its thatched cottages, some made of chalk blocks, nestles at the foot of the downs along the spring-line. The Church of St Mary the Virgin dates from the 12th century, although there have been many alterations over the years. In the chancel is a memorial to Thomas Stock (1749–1803). It was in the church that, as curate in 1777, he started his Sunday School classes for children, which were the UK's first.

At the top of the lane, with St Mary's Church ahead, bear right and then left immediately after a house following the surfaced path just to the right of the churchyard. Follow the path as it swings right and then enter a field. Follow the right-hand boundary, cross a track and keep ahead through bushes before following the right-hand field margin straight on. Pass to the left of a small reservoir hidden by bushes and continue through the next field, following the grassy strip for 175m before bearing half-right down across the field. Go down the bank, cross the road and take the path just to the right of the driveway.

Head down across two fields and leave over a stile in the lower-left corner. Follow the lane through **Idstone** as it curves left, and then keep right at the junction for 75m to reach Lower Idstone Farm.

Turn left through the farmyard past the barns, then cross a stile. Continue across the field, and shortly follow the right-hand hedge to the far corner. Go through gates either side of the footbridge and continue for 600m, following the left-hand hedge and then an enclosed grassy track. Turn right along the lane to a T-junction and then turn left. At the split take the right-hand fork (Cues Lane), and where this turns left go straight on past the thatch-roofed Cues Farm House. Ignore the first footbridge on the

The Royal Oak pub at Bishopstone

Thatched cottages overlook the pond at Bishopstone

To visit The Royal Oak pub turn left along the main road and then left along Cues Lane for 100m.

right and turn right over the second. Follow the path up into the churchyard and bear left to leave through a gate. Follow the gravel driveway to a road in **Bishopstone**. ◄

> Tucked below the downs, picturesque thatched cottages huddle round the village pond in **Bishopstone**. Step inside the Church of St Mary the Virgin, which dates from Norman times, to see an old clock mechanism from 1654 and a colourful stained-glass memorial window.

Cross over the road and follow Oxon Place, with the pond on left, for 100m. Turn left and follow the narrow surfaced path, signposted for 'The City', that skirts round the pond overlooked by picturesque thatched cottages. Turn right at the third junction and go up to a road at a junction.

Turn right up Nell Road, signposted to Russley Downs, and after 50m (at the speed sign) fork right along the track, later a path through bushes. Go through gates either side of a field and follow the steep-sided coombe as it curves left and right heading uphill to a gate at the top.

Admire the view before turning left along the Ridgeway, which is followed for 3.2km back to the start, passing **Ridgeway Farm** and ignoring all crossing routes.

MARLBOROUGH
DOWNS

The impressive Iron Age earthworks of Barbury Castle, passed on Walk 16

WALK 13
Ramsbury and Littlecote

Start/finish	The Square in Ramsbury, off the B4192 to the west of Hungerford (SU 275 715); on-street parking nearby
Distance	10.3km (6½ miles)
Ascent	165m
Time	3hr
Maps	OS Explorer 157 and 158
Refreshments	The Bell (01672 520230), Crown and Anchor (01672 520335) and shops at Ramsbury
Public transport	Ramsbury has bus links to Swindon, Marlborough and Hungerford (except Sundays)

An easy walk along the Kennet Valley based around the picturesque village of Ramsbury, once a busy place on the old coaching route between London and Bristol. After leaving Ramsbury the walk heads east along the Kennet Valley – be sure to make time for a short detour on the way to see an impressive Roman mosaic. After passing historic Littlecote House the walk swings back westwards and takes a slightly higher route back to Ramsbury.

At the fire station a path on left gives access to the Ramsbury Meadow Nature Reserve.

From The Square in **Ramsbury**, overlooked by The Bell pub, follow the High Street westwards for 500m, passing the Church of the Holy Cross on the way. ◀

Peaceful **Ramsbury** used to be on the main coaching route from London to the west; however, the present A4 takes a more direct route that bypasses the village. The village had a tradition for making beer, and in the late 18th century it was mentioned in the Wiltshire Directory that 'Ramsbury is noted for the excellent beer of which there is a great consumption in London'; recently the tradition has been revived with the opening of the Ramsbury Brewery.

Inside the Church of the Holy Cross is an interesting collection of memorials, including some by the sculptor Peter Matthias Van Gelder; unfortunately, the brass memorials in the Darrell Chapel have been 'lost' over the centuries. However, it is the Saxon remains from the original church that are the main draw, including a beautiful font complete with carved fish, parts of two carved crosses and two grave covers.

Where the road swings right, turn left along Mill Lane to its end. Keep ahead across two footbridges crossing the River Kennet

The Saxon font at the Church of the Holy Cross in Ramsbury

RAF Ramsbury, a former Second World War airfield, was located on the flat top of Springs Hill up to the right.

and follow the track ahead. Go between two thatched cottages, following the track as it curves left; continue along the track for 800m. ◀

Cross straight over the minor road and follow the surfaced driveway. Where this curves right, go straight on along the track for 1km to reach West Lodge. Continue along the narrow bridleway, later following the field edge to a track junction, where the main route goes straight on. To visit Littlecote **Roman villa**, turn left and follow the track as it curves left to a wooden building covering the mosaic floor; retrace steps and turn left.

The remains of the **Roman villa**, which include a mosaic floor – the Orpheus mosaic – dating from AD360, were first discovered in 1727. However, despite being described at the time as 'the finest pavement that the sun ever shone upon in England', it was reburied in 1730 and later declared lost. However, the story does not end there, for in 1977 the mosaic was rediscovered and fully restored. In the centre of the mosaic is Orpheus – musician and priest to Apollo, the sun god – surrounded by four goddesses representing the four seasons.

Part of the lovely Roman mosaic at Littlecote

Continue along the tree-lined track and then the surfaced driveway for 800m, passing to the right of **Littlecote House**.

> **Littlecote House**, reputedly where Henry VIII met Jane Seymour, his third wife, was originally built in the 13th century by the de Calstone family. It then passed through marriage to the Darrells in 1415, and it was the Darrells who built the present early 16th-century Tudor mansion. The last Darrell at Littlecote was William, often referred to as 'Wild Darrell' as he was allegedly connected with several scandals.
>
> Sir John Popham, one-time Lord Chief Justice of England who presided over the trials of Sir Walter Raleigh in 1603 and Guy Fawkes (of Gunpowder Plot fame) in 1606, acquired Littlecote in 1589. He was responsible for the late Elizabethan south facade of the present mansion.
>
> The house then stayed with the family until 1929, when Sir Ernest Salter Wills bought the house; the family had made their fortune in tobacco. During the Second World War, US soldiers were stationed at the house, and The Kennet Valley at War Trust has been granted the use of a room in the house as a small museum. Littlecote is now a country house hotel and leisure resort (to visit the museum contact the hotel on 01488 682509).

Keep ahead through the gated entrance and immediately turn sharp right up along the minor road for 600m. At the left-hand bend go straight on along the entrance driveway, and where this turns down to the right (back to Littlecote House) keep ahead along the track. After 500m, where the main track curves right, go straight on past a gate following the left-hand field edge. Later there is a line of beech trees on the right and open field on the left. Follow the track through the trees to a junction, and keep left for 150m alongside the trees to another junction. Turn right (north-west) following the bridleway up

The return route meanders past Whitehill Coppice

across the field and go straight on through the trees of Great Coppice (a great place for bluebells in late spring). Keep ahead down across the grassy slope to a three-way track junction. Follow the concrete track northwards uphill, and where this turns right go straight on along the sunken bridleway through Whitehill Coppice – marked as **Park Coppice** on the map extract – (another wood with bluebells).

For a more direct route (missing out the Crown and Anchor pub) turn left at the T-junction and follow the pavement back to The Square.

Continue downhill, passing a seat with a view across the valley, and at the junction turn left back along the surfaced driveway passed earlier in the walk. Turn right along the minor road towards Ramsbury crossing the **River Kennet**. At the T-junction go right and then left across the road and up Union Street to a crossroads beside the Crown and Anchor pub. ◄

Turn left down Oxford Street, passing a shop and thatched cottages back to The Square.

WALK 14

Mildenhall and the River Kennet

Start/finish	The Horseshoe Inn at Mildenhall (SU 210 696); limited on-street parking in village
Distance	8.3km (5¼ miles)
Ascent	125m
Time	2¼hr
Map	OS Explorer 157
Refreshments	The Horseshoe Inn (01672 514725) at Mildenhall
Public transport	Buses between Marlborough and Swindon stop at Mildenhall (excluding Sundays)

From the picturesque former Saxon settlement of Mildenhall the walk heads east along the Kennet Valley, passing close to the site of the former Roman town of Cunetio to arrive at Stitchcombe. Here the route rises up the side of the valley before heading east, with some lovely views over the valley, and finally dropping back down to Mildenhall, passing the historic village church on the way.

Stand facing the thatch-roofed Horseshoe Inn and turn right (east) to head along the main street through **Mildenhall**. At the junction (beside a phone box), keep right along the main road, and at the next junction turn right. Follow

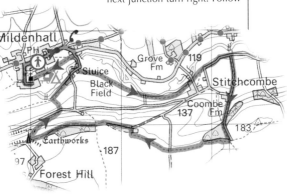

The River Kennet at Mildenhall

the lane across the picturesque **River Kennet**, and just after the right-hand bend turn left over a stile and follow a path signposted to Stitchcombe.

The 45-mile-long **River Kennet** – one of the great chalk rivers of southern England – rises at several locations, including Swallowhead Springs near Silbury Hill (Walk 18), and flows eastwards to join the River Thames at Reading.

Follow the right-hand hedge for 800m through the meadow; beyond the hedge is **Black Field**, site of the former Roman fortified settlement of Cunetio.

Cunetio was built at the crossing of several Roman roads that ran between Londinium (London) and Aquae Sulis (Bath) – north lead to Durocornovium (near Swindon), while another road headed southeast through Savernake Forest en route to Venta Bulgarum (Winchester). After the Romans left, Cunetio – unlike other Roman towns – was completely abandoned, with no visible signs that it ever existed except for cropmarks in aerial photographs. However, the site has revealed some interesting finds, including the Cunetio Hoard, the largest collection of Roman coins ever found in Britain (almost 55,000 coins).

At the end of the field cross a stile and keep ahead with the River Kennet on the left, pass some trees and later continue along an enclosed path with a house on the right.

At **Stitchcombe** cross the lane diagonally left, go over the stile and continue through the field, aiming for a telegraph pole. Cross a stile on the opposite side and follow the lane straight on for 300m to reach a crossing path and turn right. ▶

About 75m to the left is a picturesque spot beside the River Kennet.

Pass two gates and follow the enclosed grassy track through two more gates past **Coombe Farm**. Continue up along the track to a path junction at a gate. Turn right over

The route down Forest Hill gives a good view across the valley

Take a moment to admire the view, with Marlborough to the west and the Church of St John the Baptist at Mildenhall to the north.

two stiles just before the gate and head west through the field with Oxleaze Wood on the right. Continue along the field margin and go straight over the minor road. Cross the stile and continue along the margin of the right-hand field for 400m. Turn right, following a track past Hill Barn (derelict) to a track junction, and turn left for 150m. At the slight left-hand bend, fork right into the field and continue with the trees on the left and a view across the valley on the right.

Keep ahead at the crossing track (Cock-a-troop Lane), still following the left-hand field boundary towards a communication mast on **Forest Hill**. At the top-left corner go through a gate and turn sharp right heading north-east diagonally down the slope (open access land), following the trees on the right at first and later passing a wooden electricity pole. ◀

At the bottom of the slope cross a stile, bear right along the lane (Chopping Knife Lane) for 25m and then go left at a gate and stile. Follow the hedge-lined track down to a path junction and turn right along the tree-shaded path, later keeping ahead along the track with cottages on the right. Bear left along the lane (Cock-a-troop Lane), passing the stile crossed earlier, and bear left to recross the River Kennet.

After the first house entrance on the left, turn left along the enclosed path and keep ahead past the cricket ground following the left-hand fence. Continue through two fields separated by a gate, aiming for the Church of St John the Baptist in Mildenhall. Go through two gates and follow the surfaced path through the churchyard, passing to the left of the church.

The picturesque village of **Mildenhall**, pronounced and sometimes written as 'Minal', lies just to the east of Marlborough. The Church of St John the Baptist dates back to Saxon times; look closely at the lower parts of the tower and there are traces of Saxon stonework and a blocked-up window. While outside take a look at the sundial, which shows the local time – 7 minutes behind Greenwich Mean Time.

Inside the church, six main arches and corresponding large columns in the nave date from the 12th century, while in the east window are fragments of stained glass claimed to be some of the oldest in Wiltshire. However, it is the magnificent Georgian woodwork that makes Mildenhall's church exceptional. In 1816, twelve wealthy parishioners funded the refurbishment of the interior that we see today, with beautiful shoulder-high box pews, matching pulpit and reading desk, and a semi-circular gallery at the west end. Sir John Betjeman referred to it as 'a church of a Jane Austen novel' having 'a forest of magnificent oak joinery, an ocean of box pews stretching shoulder high all over the church'.

Leave through the lychgate and continue along Church Lane as it swings right up to a junction and turn right back to the start.

WALK 15
Marlborough and Savernake Forest

Start/finish	Town Hall at the east end of the High Street (A4) in Marlborough (SU 188 691); pay and display parking in George Lane off the High Street
Distance	12km (7½ miles) or (including Savernake Forest) 19.3km (12 miles)
Ascent	240m or 340m
Time	3½hrs or 5½hrs
Map	OS Explorer 157
Refreshments	Lots of choice in Marlborough
Public transport	Marlborough has daily bus services from Swindon, Pewsey and Salisbury; also services from Hungerford and Great Bedwyn (excluding Sundays)

From historic Marlborough the walk meanders south through open farmland before heading into Savernake Forest, a tranquil remnant of a much larger royal hunting ground. The walk then heads back to Marlborough following part of a disused railway before crossing the River Kennet back to the start. An optional longer route takes in more of the beech- and oak-wooded Savernake Forest and visits a distinctive monument.

The Town Hall at the east end of Marlborough's wide High Street

MARLBOROUGH

The market town of Marlborough, once a staging post on the old coach route from London to Bristol (now the A4), is home to one of the widest high streets in Britain and a famous college. Former college pupils include Kate Middleton (now HRH The Duchess of Cambridge), the engineer Sir Nigel Gresley (designer of the famous Flying Scotsman and Mallard steam trains) and the yachtsman Sir Francis Chichester (who circumnavigated the globe in Gypsy Moth VI).

First mentioned in the Domesday Book as 'Merleberge', Marlborough can trace its origins back over 4000 years. Lying within the private grounds of the college is a small hill once used as part of a Norman castle. However, recent carbon dating has found that the mound was made around 2400BC and is a smaller version of Silbury Hill (Walk 18).

At the eastern end of the High Street, beyond the Victorian Town Hall, is St Mary's Church and The Green. Overlooking The Green is the house (blue plaque) where William Golding, author of *Lord of the Flies* (1954), lived while his father taught at Marlborough Grammar School. At the western end is the 15th-century Church of St Peter and St Paul. In 1498 Thomas Wolsey, later Cardinal Wolsey and Lord Chancellor for Henry VIII, was ordained as a priest here. The church is now a community centre and café. In between are several interesting buildings, including the tile-hung 17th-century Merchant's House (01672 511690).

Follow the south side of the High Street heading south-west, later passing to the left of the Church of St Peter and St Paul, to a roundabout and turn left (**A345**) along the pavement. Cross the road at the River Kennet bridge, keep ahead and turn right on a track (bridleway and White Horse Trail) at the mini-roundabout. Follow the track for 800m, with the **River Kennet** on the right and then a sports ground on the left. ▶ After the tennis courts turn left; to the right is **Preshute House** and St George's Church.

Follow the enclosed path, go through a gate and up through two fields to the upper boundary. Cross a stile and continue along the enclosed route, crossing another stile on the way. At the end, cross a stile and bear left across the main road (A345). Take the surfaced track opposite and, where this swings right, go straight on under the disused

Look left for a glimpse of the diminutive Marlborough, or Preshute, White Horse, which was cut in 1804.

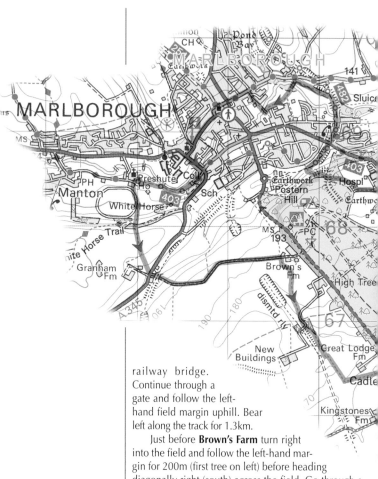

railway bridge. Continue through a gate and follow the left-hand field margin uphill. Bear left along the track for 1.3km.

Just before **Brown's Farm** turn right into the field and follow the left-hand margin for 200m (first tree on left) before heading diagonally right (south) across the field. Go through a hedge gap and continue through the next field. Leave through a gate and bear right down the track. Where this turns sharp right (to cross the disused railway) go straight on over a stile and follow the left-hand field margin for 175m. In the next field bear right up along the right-hand field edge. At the end of the field turn left for 30m, then turn right past a solitary tree before descending to a dip.

In the next field bear diagonally left (eastwards) across the field passing to the right of **Great Lodge Farm**. Cross a stile and continue across the field in the same direction towards **Cadley**, passing just left of some trees. Go through the gate and follow the gravel track past the houses. Cross the **A346**, follow the surfaced drive-way northwards for 20m and then bear left along a grassy path with the church (private house) over to the right.

Follow the bridleway through the trees of Savernake Forest to a junction (SU 208 667); here either carry on along the main route or take the forest extension (see below – additional 7.3km/4½ miles; 1½hrs).

The medieval royal hunting ground of **Savernake Forest**, mentioned in a Saxon charter in AD934, originally stretched from East Kennett to Hungerford. William the Conqueror gave Savernake to one of his knights, and it has passed in an unbroken line for over 30 generations. Although privately owned, it has been leased to the Forestry Commission and walkers can explore most of the forest, which contains a number of ancient trees (some of which are named) as well as an interesting mix of wildlife.

Here the longer route rejoins the main route from the right.

On the main route, turn left for a few metres, then go right following the path (Church Walk) downhill to an open grassy area. Fork left heading uphill, and at the next split take the right-hand fork. Continue to rise to a crossing route (SU 208 672) and go straight over. ◄

The distinctive urn-topped Ailesbury Column

Savernake Forest extension
Turn right for 250m and keep ahead along the gravel track for 500m to a junction at a dip (SU 216 667). Turn right (south) and follow the track (New Road Bottom) ahead for 1.4km; after 300m, about 50m to the right is the Spiral Oak. Keep to the track as it swings left and continue south-eastwards for 1.5km (after 500m passing Bitham Pool, one of several ponds in the forest) to a track junction with a distinctive tall **column** opposite and turn left. The urn-topped Ailesbury Column was erected in 1781 by Thomas Bruce, Earl of Ailesbury, who lived at nearby Tottenham House.

After 25m turn left again and follow the track (Charcoal Burners Road) for 500m to a cross-track junction. Turn right, following Twelve O'Clock Drive north for 1.6km to a junction of eight tracks at **Eight Walks** (after 350m on the left is the Turkey Oak). Take the second track on the left (Great Lodge Drive) for 900m back to the junction (SU 216 667) passed earlier. Turn right and follow the narrow path northwards for 450m. At the path junction before **Braydon Hook**, turn left. Ignore a crossing path and head gently uphill to a cross-junction (SU 208 672); turn right to rejoin the main walk.

To continue the main walk follow the bridleway northwards for 650m, passing Old Paunchy (a bulbous old oak tree over to the left) on the way. Bear right along the gravel track near **Furze Coppice** and keep ahead at the junction. Just before the road (**A4**) turn left, following a bridleway alongside the fence on the left (road on the right) to a surfaced track (signposted for the Marlborough Cricket and Hockey Club) and turn left. ▸

To the right, across the A4, is a former toll house – people had to pay a toll to travel through the Savernake estate.

Keep left at the split to reach the cricket ground. Follow the track at it swings right behind the clubhouse, and at the end of the car park turn left over a v-stile. Bear right through the trees and keep left at the split, cross an old earthwork and keep left to reach a crossing path. Turn sharp right down Postern Hill and pass under the line of wooden electricity poles to reach a signed path junction. Turn right along the old railway embankment for 850m, passing under the A4 and then crossing bridges over a lane and the River Kennet. ▸

The former 19th-century Swindon, Marlborough & Andover Railway embankment now forms a path and cycleway between Marlborough and Chiseldon.

At the crossing path turn left down steps, go through a gate and head west-north-west (left fork, parallel to river) through the field for 300m. Turn left, cross the River Kennet and continue, heading south-south-west along the grassy path for 150m towards a building; the route is now passing through Stonebridge Wild River Reserve, which has a number of paths and boardwalks giving access to water meadow and riverbank habitats. At the junction bear right, still following the grassy path with a hedge on

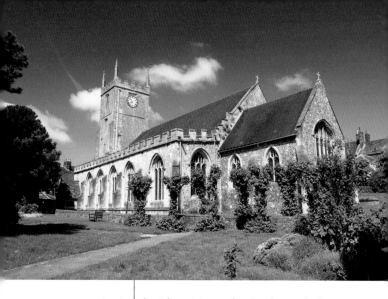

St Mary's Church, Marlborough

the right, to join a surfaced path (Stonebridge Lane). Turn right and cross the footbridge over the River Kennet.

Follow the path up to a road and turn left to a cross-roads. Cross the A346 at the traffic lights and follow the tree-lined surfaced path across The Green. Keep ahead past a house (blue plaque to the author William Golding) and then St Mary's Church. Go through the archway and bear left back to the start.

Parts of **St Mary's Church** date back to the 12th century. In 1642, during the English Civil War, Marlborough was under a Royalist siege. The Parliamentarian commander took refuge in the church, and the north side of the tower still bears the marks of shot from Royalist guns.

WALK 16

Ogbourne St Andrew, Rockley
and Barbury Castle

Start/finish	War memorial beside the A346 in Ogbourne St Andrew (SU 190 721); on-street parking in village. Alternative parking/start: Hackpen Hill (SU 128 747) or Barbury Castle (SU 157 760)
Distance	20.6km (12¾ miles) or (via Four Mile Clump) 12.4km (7¾ miles)
Ascent	335m or 220m
Time	5¾ or 3½hr
Map	OS Explorer 157
Refreshments	The Silks on the Downs pub (01672 841229) at Ogbourne St Andrew; The Inn with the Well (01672 841445) at Ogbourne St George (off route)
Public transport	Daily bus services between Swindon and Salisbury stop at Ogbourne St Andrew (A346). (To join the route from the bus stop, follow the A346 past The Silks on the Downs pub to reach the war memorial.)

This full-day walk starts from Ogbourne St Andrew and passes through the little hamlet of Rockley before climbing up to join the Ridgeway. The walk then follows a section of this National Trail, offering some great views as it passes the Iron Age earthworks of Barbury Castle and then takes in a sweeping descent along Smeathe's Ridge. The final section returns along the valley of the River Og. A shorter walk is also described.

Ogbourne St Andrew, along with neighbouring **Ogbourne St George**, has a long history stretching back to Saxon times. In the 12th century the manorial rights of Great and Little Ogbourne (now Ogbourne St George and Ogbourne St Andrew) were donated by Maud of Wallingford to the Benedictine Abbey of Bec-Helloin in Normandy. Almost 300 years later, during the reign of Henry V,

all alien orders were suppressed, and the estate passed to the Duke of Bedford in 1422 before passing to the Crown on his death. During the reign of Henry VI the land was granted to King's College in Cambridge, and was held by them until 1927.

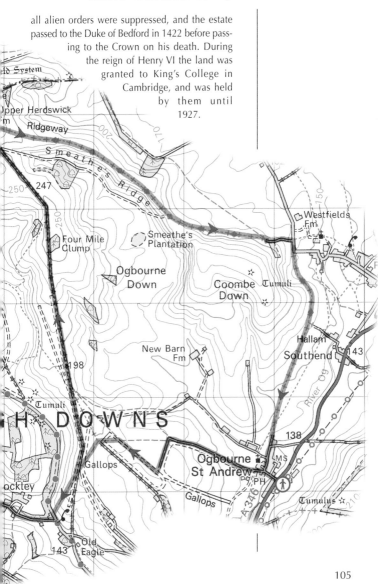

From the war memorial follow the village street for 175m, heading away from the **A346** to a junction and fork left. At the next split take the right-hand track straight on for 1km up to a junction. Turn left to a fence and go right, following a grassy track beside a hedge (right), with gallops to the left, for 500m. Bear half-left through a gap in the fence, head west across the gallop and leave through a gap in the corner. Keep ahead through the bushes to a track (SU 170 725).

Short-cut via Four Mile Clump

Turn right (north) along the track for 3.6km, later passing **Four Mile Clump**, and just before Upper Herdswick Farm turn right through a gate to rejoin the main walk (this point is indicated in the sidebar on page 109).

The main walk goes over the track and follows the bridleway south-westwards between the bushes (left) and fence (right) for 300m (with a gate ahead). Turn right through a gap in the fence, head across the gallop and through a gate. Turn left along the track, and after 120m bear right over the gallop and follow the fence to a gate in the far-right corner. Go through this and head down across the field before leaving through another gate. Cross the road

Crossing gallops on the way to Rockley

and follow the lane opposite for 800m through **Rockley**, passing cottages and a duck pond.

At the four-way junction turn left following the tree-shaded track (bridleway) uphill. After 500m dogleg left into a field and continue along the right-hand boundary to a track. Turn right for 100m to a split and take the right-hand fork gently uphill, with a small wood (The Beeches) on the right. Keep ahead through a gate and continue across the grassy field strewn with **sarsen stones** towards the trees.

Sarsen Stones, known locally as 'grey wethers', as from a distance they look like sheep (a 'wether' is a castrated ram), are all that remains of a hard silica sandstone layer that was formed over the underlying chalk during the early Tertiary period, 50 million years ago. Subsequent erosion broke the layer into pieces, creating the sarsens. Used in ancient times for building purposes, today they support communities of rare lichen and moss.

Later bear right along a grassy track (White Horse Trail). Go through a gate and continue through Totterdown Wood following the White Horse Trail. ▶ On leaving the wood keep ahead along the hedged route to a crossing track. Cross over and continue along the enclosed route heading north and then north-west. After 600m keep left at a split and then turn right still following the hedge (scrub and trees on right). Keep ahead to join the Ridgeway beside Berwick Bassett dewpond and bear right (north); the walk now follows the Ridgeway for 10.5km.

After 1.8km the route crosses a minor road on **Hackpen Hill** (alternative parking/start); immediately before this a short detour through the gate on the left leads to a **white-horse hill figure**.

This 145km (90 mile) trail meanders through Wiltshire visiting eight white-horse hill figures.

The **Hackpen** (or Broad Hinton) **White Horse** was cut by Henry Eatwell, Parish Clerk of Broad Hinton and a local publican, to commemorate the Coronation of Queen Victoria in 1838.

Continue along the Ridgeway, passing three picturesque circular beech copses (left); shortly the earthworks of Barbury Castle come into view. Drop down to a minor road, turn right for 40m and then left through the gate, following the track uphill and soon passing through the earthworks of **Barbury Castle**.

The imposing Iron Age earthworks of **Barbury Castle**, built 2500 years ago, are said to be the location of the Battle of Beranburgh (Beran Byrig), where the Saxons defeated the Britons in AD556.

The surrounding landscape has inspired many, including two **local writers** – Richard Jefferies (1848–1887), noted for his depiction of English rural life, and Alfred Williams (1877–1930). Williams was dubbed 'the hammerman poet' as he used to work in the Great Western Railway Factory at Swindon (memorial stone on Burderop Down at SU 158 672).

To the north is the former Second World War **Wroughton Airfield**. The six hangars have been home to parts of the British Science Museum since the 1970s.

Following the Ridgeway towards Ogbourne St George

Continue through the centre of the hill fort, although a short detour along the ramparts is worth it for the views. Pass through the eastern side of the earthworks and continue following the Ridgeway in a south-easterly direction past the car park (alternative parking/start). On reaching the surfaced track at **Upper Herdswick Farm** turn right for 200m, then left through a gate. ▶

The shorter walk rejoins the main route here.

Follow the Ridgeway along the broad outline of **Smeathe's Ridge** in a south-easterly direction, with lovely views across the Marlborough Downs. On reaching a gateway and cattle grid (SU 175 752) admire the view before continuing down alongside the fence to a dip. Go on for a short distance before forking left at the marker and following a grassy track downhill to pass through a gate. Keep straight on towards **Ogbourne St George** to join a road.

> To visit **Ogbourne St George** cross the road, go through the trees and cross two stiles. Keep ahead across the field and then through the churchyard. Go right along the lane and turn left up the main street to the T-junction (to the left is The Inn with the Well), then retrace your steps to return to the main route (1.2km each way). Inside the 12th-century church, which underwent extensive Victorian renovations, there is an early 16th-century brass memorial to Thomas Goddard and his wife.

Turn right, and as the road curves left go straight on along the track signposted 'Ridgeway to Liddington Castle'. At the junction, where the Ridgeway goes left, go straight on along the byway to **Ogbourne St Andrew**. Keep ahead along the lane; a junction on the right gives access to the 12th-century St Andrew's Church (inside are several interesting memorials, including two 17th-century ones to members of the Goddard family). Continue through the village following the street as it curves left back to the start.

WALK 17
Fyfield Down and the Devil's Den

Start/finish	Car park south of Manton House (SU 159 699); access via minor road signposted to Manton, west of Marlborough off the A4
Alternative start/finish	Fyfield (SU 147 687)
Distance	12.1km (7½ miles) or (shorter route) 7.2km (4½ miles); Fyfield start/finish add 2.5km (1½ miles)
Ascent	175m or 105m; Fyfield start/finish add 75m
Time	3½hr or 2hr; Fyfield start/finish add ¾hr
Map	OS Explorer 157
Refreshments	None on walk; large choice in Marlborough
Public transport	Buses between Marlborough and Calne stop at Fyfield (SU 146 686, off route), excluding Sundays

---

This walk, to the east of Avebury, follows short sections of two trails – the White Horse Trail and the Ridgeway – and explores the strange, sarsen-strewn landscape of Fyfield Down National Nature Reserve. Near the end, a short loop takes in a visit of the Devil's Den. A shorter version of the walk is also described.

Alternative start from Fyfield

From the north side of the A4 in **Fyfield**, opposite the road signposted to Lower Fyfield and church, head north up the tarmac track (bridleway). At **Fyfield Hill** follow the track as it curves left past the buildings for 20m and then turn right (north) down the hedge-lined bridleway. Go through a gate to reach the main route by some trees (SU 146 700); this point is indicated in sidebar on page 113. Turn right onto the main route.

The walk follows the White Horse Trail for 4.7km.

From the south-west corner of the car park follow the track signposted to Avebury and Hackpen heading west-north-west. ◄ After 600m continue along the track, ignoring a bridleway to the left (this is the return route), heading north-westwards for 1.4km over **Clatford Down** to a track junction beside a covered **reservoir**.

Shorter route

Turn left and follow the track for 800m to a gate (SU 136 711); turn left to rejoin the main walk (this point is indicated in the sidebar on page 113).

Turn left along the Herepath (Green Street) for 75m, and then turn right through a gate. ▶ Continue north-westwards alongside the trees (right) and then keep ahead across the field. Go through a gate and continue through Totterdown Wood. Keep ahead between the hedge (left) and trees to a crossing track with a cattle grid on the left. Go straight on, following the enclosed route heading north and then north-west. Keep to the White Horse Trail as it skirts clockwise round some trees (ignore a bridleway to right and left) before

The Herepath (rejoined later in the walk) is an Anglo-Saxon army route – 'herepath' means 'army path'.

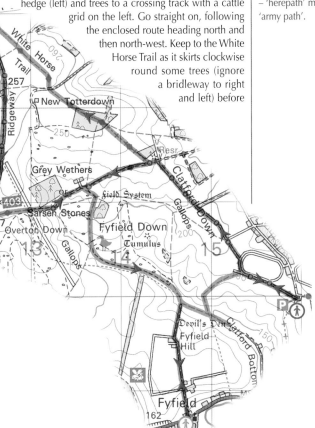

111

The first part of the walk follows the White Horse Trail

continuing to join the Ridgeway beside Berwick Bassett dewpond.

Turn left and follow the Ridgeway southwards for 2.1km. A seat on the way provides a lovely view to the west over Monkton Down, which includes Avebury (Walk 18) and the more distant Lansdowne Monument on Cherhill Down (Walk 19). After 1.4km a gate on the left (SU 126 715) allows for a short detour (200m each way) to the polissoir, or polishing stone.

To visit the polissoir turn left through the gate to enter the open access land. Follow the fence on the left for 150m and then turn right for 50m to a large, flat sarsen stone beside some gorse bushes (SU 128 715; GPS: 51.44239, -1.81672). Retrace your steps to rejoin the main route.

The stone, or **polissoir**, displays several grooves and a smoothed area that were formed by Neolithic people as they sharpened and polished their stone axes several thousand years ago.

The main route continues along the Ridgeway to a junction (SU 124 708; to the right is Avebury) with the Herepath (Wessex Ridgeway). Turn left through the gate, passing a sign for Fyfield Down National Nature Reserve (NNR). Head eastwards across the open grass and go through gates either side of a gallop before following the track just south of Delling Copse, with a great view across the sarsen-strewn landscape. ▶

The nationally important geological site of Fyfield Down contains around 25,000 sarsen stones that support rare lichen communities (see also Walk 16).

Keep to the gravel track close to Delling Copse, go through a gate and turn right. ▶ Follow the right-hand fence for 175m, turn right through the first gate and follow the fence on the left, with Wroughton Copse beyond, for 450m heading south. Go through a gate to enter the open access land and follow a path along the valley floor, passing areas of sarsen stones for 1.4km; the right of way follows the right-hand boundary. After 1.1km there is a stand of trees on the right. ▶

The shorter walk rejoins the main route here.

The alternative route from Fyfield joins/ leaves the main route here.

On reaching a gate at the south-eastern edge of the open access land the walk turns up to the left; however, before that it follows a short loop to the Devil's Den.

The Devil's Den

Keep ahead through the gate and follow the bridleway for 250m before turning right through a gate to enter a small field in which stands the **Devil's Den** (note: access to the field containing the Devil's Den is provided on a permissive basis – please observe any changes).

The three large sarsen stones known as the **Devil's Den** are the remains of a Neolithic long barrow or burial mound. From an illustration by William Stukeley in 1723, we know that there were other sarsens arranged along the sides of the mound, although these have long since disappeared. The great Wessex novelist Thomas Hardy referred to it as the 'Devil's Door' in his short story *What the Shepherd Saw* (1881), in which he described it as 'a Druidical trilithon, consisting of three oblong stones in the form of a doorway, two on end, and one across as a lintel…locally called the Devil's Door'.

Retrace steps back to the open access land and turn right, heading north up beside the fence, and soon bear right, still rising and following the fence. Go through a gate at the far-right corner and bear right along the track back to the car park.

WALK 18

Avebury

Start/finish	Overton Hill car park on the A4 (SU 118 680) between West Overton and Beckhampton
Distance	11.2km (7 miles) or (via West Kennet Avenue) 11.5km (7¼ miles)
Ascent	165m or 205m
Time	3hr or 3¼hr
Map	OS Explorer 157
Refreshments	The Red Lion (01672 539266), shop and café at Avebury
Public transport	Daily bus services to Avebury from Swindon and Devizes and from Marlborough and Calne (excluding Sundays)

This walk explores some of the most impressive prehistoric sites in Britain, which form part of a World Heritage Site. From Overton Hill the walk heads north, past Bronze Age burial mounds, and follows a short section of the Ridgeway before turning south-west towards Avebury and passing through the spectacular henge earthworks. The walk then continues south past mysterious Silbury Hill before reaching West Kennett Long Barrow – one of the largest and best preserved long barrows in Britain. The final section meanders through East Kennett before passing The Sanctuary, site of a prehistoric timber and stone circle, and returning to Overton Hill. An alternative route from Avebury follows a section of the West Kennet Avenue, a double line of standing stones that once ran between the henge and The Sanctuary.

Head north along the Ridgeway (track) from **Overton Hill** car park. A sign mentions it is 139km (87 miles) to Ivinghoe Beacon – however, your walk follows the Ridgeway for just 2.8km to a junction (SU 125 708) on **Overton Down**. ▶

The path to the east leads to the sarsen-strewn landscape of Fyfield Down NNR (Walk 17).

On the right at **Overton Hill** are several well-preserved early Bronze Age (about 2000BC) burial mounds or round barrows. Much later a Roman

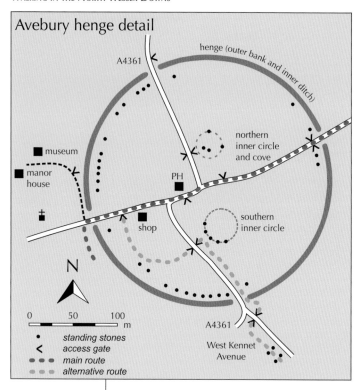

Avebury henge detail

road between Cunetio (near Marlborough) and Verlicio (near Chippenham) passed through here. To the west of the Ridgeway are several tree-crowned burial mounds that are known locally as 'hedgehogs'.

Turn left (south-west) along the Herepath (or Green Street), which is also the **Wessex Ridgeway**, heading towards Avebury. After **Manor Farm** the track becomes a tarmac lane and soon passes through the henge earthworks (gates gives access either side) at **Avebury**. At the main road keep ahead past the reputedly haunted 400-year-old

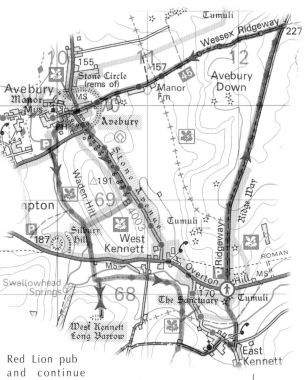

Red Lion pub
and continue
along the High Street. Shortly after
the village shop turn left along the enclosed path (White
Horse Trail). ▶ A track to the right leads to Avebury
Manor, the Alexander Keiller Museum and café; further
along the High Street is St James' Church which, although
altered by the Normans, still retains its Anglo-Saxon nave.

The alternative route
via West Kennet
Avenue (see below)
turns left through a
gate immediately
after the shop.

Dating from 2600ʙᴄ, the most impressive feature at
Avebury is the large **henge**. This type of Neolithic
earthwork consists of a circular or oval outer bank
and an inner ditch (unlike a defensive Iron Age
hill fort, which has an inner bank and outer ditch).
Within this structure is an outer stone circle, one
of Europe's largest stone circles, originally marked
with 98 sarsen stones, as well as two smaller stone

Take time to explore the stone circle and henge at Avebury

circles and part of the present village. Along with Stonehenge, the Avebury henge and associated sites have been designated a World Heritage Site. Linking the henge with The Sanctuary (see below) is the West Kennet Avenue, which originally consisted of 100 pairs of standing stones.

The **Alexander Keiller Museum**, which houses archaeological finds from the area, is named after Alexander Keiller (1889–1955), heir to the Dundee-based marmalade business, who was responsible for excavating many of the sites at Avebury in the 1930s. Nearby is the 16th-century Manor House that was once the home of Alexander Keiller (01672 539250).

Alternative route via West Kennet Avenue

Just after passing the shop (but before the waymarked footpath) turn left through a gate and follow the path as it curves left near the stones to a gate on the left. Cross the main road (**A4361**) and go through a gate opposite. Turn right to the trees and leave through a gate on the right. Cross the road (**B4003**) and go through a gate opposite. Bear left following the line of the **West Kennet Avenue** for 800m to the far left corner.

The 2.5km-long **West Kennet Avenue** was built as a link between the pre-existing henge and The Sanctuary. The avenue, which is 15m wide, originally consisted of 100 pairs of standing stones spaced every 25m. Although fewer than 30 now remain, with a similar number marked by concrete markers, the avenue remains an intriguing sight as it meanders through the open landscape.

Go through two gates to enter the adjacent field and turn right along a permissive path up **Waden Hill**; from the top admire the view including Silbury Hill. Continue downhill and turn left to rejoin the main route beside the **River Kennet**.

For the main route keep ahead through the **car park** and turn right along the **A4361** for 40m. Turn left to cross the road and go through the gate. Keep to the path beside the **River Kennet** for 1.3km; over to the right is the unmistakable outline of Silbury Hill (there is no access to the hill). ▶

The alternative route rejoins the main route here.

The 40m-high **Silbury Hill** is the largest man-made prehistoric mound in Europe, built around 2400BC (late Neolithic), at a similar time to the Avebury stone circle. No one really knows why it was built, although local legend attributes the mound to the Devil. He was planning to dump a load of earth on nearby Marlborough, but was stopped by the priests at Avebury, while in another version it's a cobbler who thwarts the Devil.

Mysterious Silbury Hill

Go through the gate and, with care, cross the **A4** and turn left for 30m and then right through the gate following a track southwards. After crossing the River Kennet – which rises at several places including near Silbury Hill – go through a gate and bear left along a path to a large oak tree (SU 104 681). Here turn right (south) following a permissive path for 400m up to the **West Kennett Long Barrow**. Dating from 3600BC, this is one of the largest and most impressive Neolithic chambered tombs in Britain. From the barrow, retrace steps to the oak tree and turn right.

Follow the fence along the left side of the field, cross a stile and continue along the track. Cross the lane and stile to follow the hedge on the right as it curves right. Cross a stile and follow the tree-shaded path to a track. Cross slightly left and go up the bridleway to another crossing track (the White Horse Trail goes straight on). Turn left down the track and follow it as it bears left between buildings at **East Kennett**. Continue along the lane past Christ Church to a T-junction.

Go right, and just before the house on the left turn left along a narrow path between the stone wall and house to a lane and then turn left. Where the lane curves right go straight on (wall on left). Cross the River Kennet and follow the track as it bears left and then right (northwards) to reach the A4; to the left is a gate giving access to **The Sanctuary**.

The Sanctuary, which dates from 3000BC, consisted of concentric timber and stone circles. We know from the writings of John Aubrey that in 1648 many of the stones were still standing; however, within 100 years the site was destroyed (the stones, like many others, were used as building material). All that remains today are concrete blocks marking where the timbers and stones once stood.

Carefully cross over the busy road (A4) back to the car park at Overton Hill.

VALE OF PEWSEY

Heading up towards the Cherhill White Horse and Oldbury Castle (Walk 19)

WALK 19

Cherhill and Oldbury Castle

Start/finish	Smallgrain car park, 3km south along the Bishops Cannings road off the A4 at Cherhill (SU 019 670)
Distance	11.2km (7 miles)
Ascent	290m
Time	3¼hr
Map	OS Explorer 157
Refreshments	The Black Horse (01249 817874) at Cherhill
Public transport	Buses between Calne and Marlborough stop at Cherhill (excluding Sundays)

The walk heads north through Calstone Wellington to Cherhill on the A4, which was once the main coaching route between London and Bristol. From here it's a stiff climb to the top of Cherhill Hill, home to a monument, white-horse hill figure, Oldbury Castle Iron Age hill fort and some great views. The route then heads down to a former Roman road that is followed back to the start.

From the north end of the car park head through the trees and turn right up the track for 450m to a gate on the left. To the north-east the monument on Cherhill Down is visible – the walk passes this later on; the gate on the right gives access to Morgan's Hill Nature Reserve (Walk 20). Turn left through two gates and follow the left-hand fence downhill through three more gates. Bear right along the track to a T-junction, turn left for 100m to the corner and turn right through a gate (note: the right of way on the map cuts diagonally across the corner of the field).

Follow the left-hand field edge for 30m, dogleg left through a gate and continue northwards, staying to the left of St Mary's Church at **Calstone Wellington**. Just beyond the church go right over a stile, and bear left along the track away from the church to a lane.

The small hamlet of **Calstone Wellington** (originally just 'Calstone') was mentioned in the Domesday Book. St Mary's Church was rebuilt in the 15th century; look inside the porch to see some 17th- and 18th-century graffiti.

Turn right along the lane to South Farm, where the lane becomes an unsurfaced track and splits. Take the left fork down through the trees, cross the bridge, and where the track bears left take the bridleway on the right-hand side up through the trees to a track. Turn right along the track, keeping straight on (left) at the junction. Continue through two fields separated by a gate to reach a junction of bridleways and a footpath beside an old barn. ▶

To miss out Cherhill: turn right up the enclosed path, keep ahead, passing left of some trees, and rejoin the main walk at a gate (SU 042 694); 1km shorter than main route.

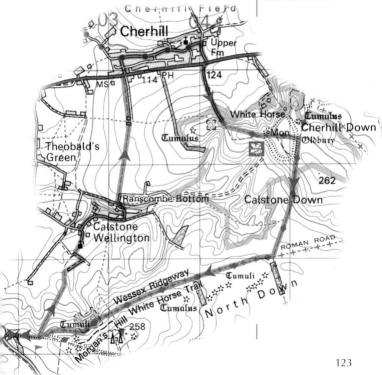

To visit The Black Horse pub turn right here and follow the A4 for 900m.

Go straight on along the track to reach the A4 at **Cherhill** and cross over the road (A4). ◄ Go north down Oliver's Hill and take the second turning on the right (The Street), heading east past some picturesque thatched cottages. At the Church of St James the Great (left), keep ahead and at the next junction turn right along Park Lane, then, with care, cross the main road (A4) diagonally right to a small lay-by.

The old coach route between London and Bristol (now the A4) ran through **Cherhill** and was the haunt of the infamous 18th-century highwaymen known as the Cherhill Gang. Inside The Black Horse pub there is a painting of the gang that shows their unusual robbing technique of not wearing a stitch of clothing, which was claimed to both startle their victims and make it harder to identify them! In spite of this, some of the gang were caught and strung up on Cherhill Hill as a warning to others.

The Church of St James the Great dates from the 12th century, and close to the church is Cherhill Manor, where in 1913 part of a fourth-century Roman mosaic floor was discovered (now located at Devizes Museum).

The earthworks of the Iron Age hill fort of Oldbury Castle crown Cherhill Hill

The Cherhill White Horse viewed from the path

Follow the bridleway uphill for 700m to a gate on the left. ▶ Bear left through the gate and follow the fence up to the prominent monument standing in the earthworks of **Oldbury Castle**, admiring the view of the white horse on the way.

The route avoiding Cherhill rejoins the main route here through a gate on the right (SU 042 694).

The two concentric banks and ditches of **Oldbury Castle** date from the Iron Age. Standing in the western corner of the fort is the **Lansdowne Monument**. This 38m-tall stone obelisk, designed by Sir Charles Barry (designer of the Houses of Parliament), was commissioned by the third Marquess of Lansdowne to commemorate his ancestor, Sir William Petty, a well-known 17th-century economist, scientist and philosopher. Just below the earthworks is the **Cherhill White Horse** that was cut in 1780 under the direction of Dr Alsop of Calne, who shouted instructions over a megaphone from the main road.

Continue eastwards from the monument, passing through the earthworks to a junction on the opposite side. Turn right, soon go through a gate and follow the route

Following a former Roman road back to the start

downhill past hawthorn bushes; views ahead include the twin masts on Morgan's Hill (Walk 20). Go through another gate and continue along the wide enclosed route to a crossing track beside a belt of trees (not the track in the field).

Turn right and follow the track for 3.1km back to the car park – noting on the left, just after the belt of trees, several tumuli in the field.

This track, part of the Wessex Ridgeway and the White Horse Trail, follows the course of a former **Roman road** that ran from Londinium (London) to Aquae Sulis (Bath) via Cunetio (Walk 14). The 220km (137 mile) **Wessex Ridgeway** runs from Marlborough to the south coast at Lyme Regis in Dorset.

WALK 20

Heddington, Oliver's Castle, Roundway
Down and Morgan's Hill

Start/finish	Smallgrain car park, 3km south along the Bishops Cannings road off the A4 at Cherhill (SU 019 670)
Distance	14km (8¾ miles)
Ascent	280m
Time	4hr
Map	OS Explorer 157
Refreshments	The Ivy Inn (01380 859652) at Heddington
Public transport	Buses between Calne and Marlborough stop at Heddington (excluding Sundays)

This walk takes in the steep scarp slope on the western fringes of the North Wessex Downs that affords some great views out across Wiltshire. The first part of the walk heads through Hampsley Hollow to visit Heddington, with its picturesque thatched pub and historic church, before skirting round Beacon Hill. After a stiff climb the walk arrives at the Iron Age earthworks of Oliver's Castle – worth a stop for the wonderful view. The walk then heads along tracks and lanes past Roundway Down, the site of an important skirmish between Parliamentarians and Royalists during the English Civil War, before following the Wansdyke over Morgan's Hill back to the start. Various parts of the walk follow sections of four long-distance routes: the Mid Wilts Way, the Wessex Ridgeway, the White Horse Trail and the Wansdyke Path.

From the north side of the car park take the path through the trees and turn left down the track. Cross over the road and bear right along the bridleway, following the field edge for 125m, then turn left between fences to a cross-junction. Turn left and follow the bridleway down to the buildings at **Hampsley Hollow**, then continue along the lane for 850m to a junction beside a house at **Heddington**.

The Ivy Inn at Heddington

Heddington, tucked below the downs, is home to the Heddington and Stockley Steam Rally and to St Andrew's Church, which dates from the 12th century.

Turn right down the lane (Hampsley Road), then left at the next junction, following Stockley Road to pass the thatch-roofed Ivy Inn. On drawing level with Home Farm (on the right just after the pub) go left through a gate in the hedge and bear half-right across the field to its corner. Then cross a stile and join Church Road, with St Andrew's Church opposite.

Turn left to a T-junction (Hampsley Road) and turn right. Follow the lane to the sharp left-hand corner at Church Farm and turn right (north-west) along the track (restricted byway). Later bear left at a cottage, heading south-west on a track, and where this turns right go straight on heading southwards to reach a crossing track.

Go straight on to another track junction. Bear left along the track for 1.4km as it skirts round **Beacon Hill** before rising up through the convoluted contours of the chalk grassland after passing a gate. At the top stay in the field and turn sharp right, following the fence on the left. Go through a gate and continue along the grassy path as it bears left towards **Oliver's Castle**.

> **Oliver's Castle** hill fort consists of a single ditch and rampart with an entrance on the eastern side. Excavations in the early 1900s

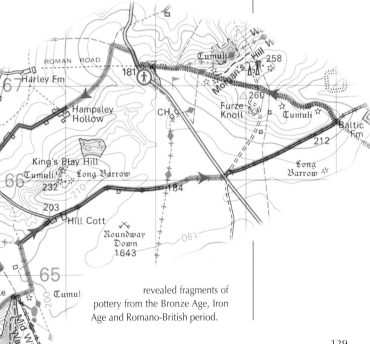

revealed fragments of pottery from the Bronze Age, Iron Age and Romano-British period.

The view across Wiltshire from Beacon Hill

The right of way heads south-south-east, following the fence on the left to a fence corner. A better option is to circle counter-clockwise round the earthworks for a fantastic view before rejoining the waymarked route at the fence corner.

Head east-north-east alongside the fence (there are parallel paths either side of the fence) to reach a gravel track and parking area. Turn right and then immediately left at the junction, following the track north-eastwards.

During the English Civil War in the 17th century a series of armed conflicts took place between Parliamentarians (Roundheads) and Royalists (Cavaliers). One such skirmish was the **Battle of Roundway Down**, fought on 13 July 1643. The Parliamentarians under Sir William Waller, who were besieging Devizes after a battle at Bath, had to withdraw to Roundway Hill to face a smaller Royalist force under Lord Wilmot. Despite being outnumbered, the Royalist forces won the day, giving them dominance in the south-west – but not for long. Today, standing

130

on these peaceful downs, it is hard to imagine that over 600 troops died here during the battle.

Follow the track as it curves left (north) and then passes a dip. At the junction bear right along the lane and keep right at the next junction beside **Hill Cottage**. Follow the track (surfaced in parts) for 2km, passing a large barn and keeping ahead at a cross-track junction to reach a road.

> These tracks once formed the **coaching route** that ran between Beckhampton (where it diverged from the main London to Bristol road, forerunner of today's A4) and Bath, passing over Beacon Hill. During the 18th century the road was turnpiked, but later fell into disuse in favour of the main London to Bristol road.

Cross over diagonally left, follow the track ahead for 20m and bear right, following the track for 1.3km to a crossing bridleway at some trees (SU 039 665). Turn left (north) through the trees and go through a gate into the field. The route now follows the Wansdyke earthwork and Wansdyke Path over **Morgan's Hill**.

> From Morgan's Hill, the **Wansdyke**, a massive linear Saxon earthwork, stretches east across the Marlborough Downs above the Vale of Pewsey as far as Marlborough. The earthwork, which dates from the late fifth century, is probably named after the Saxon god Woden; hence it became 'Woden's Dyke' and, eventually, Wansdyke. As to why it was built, opinion is divided; some suggest it was a territorial boundary, while others suggest it was a defensive structure.

Follow the Wansdyke earthwork to the masts on Morgan's Hill, twice dipping down into the ditch to go through gates. Pass to the left of the masts and keep ahead through another gate in the ditch and follow

The final part follows the Wansdyke back to the car park

the earthwork downhill through Morgan's Hill Nature Reserve – admiring the view on the way.

Morgan's Hill Nature Reserve, cared for by the Wiltshire Wildlife Trust, is home to a range of chalk grassland plants, including several orchids, as well as a number of butterflies and birds, including kestrels and yellowhammers. The name 'Morgan's Hill' is said to be derived from a local man, John Morgan, who in 1720 was hanged on the hill for murdering his uncle.

At the bottom go through a gate and bear left along the track for 350m before turning left back to the car park.

WALK 21

Alton Barnes and the Wansdyke

Start/finish	Car park near Knap Hill, 1.9km north of Alton Barnes (SU 115 638)
Distance	14.8km (9¼ miles)
Ascent	340m
Time	4¼hr
Map	OS Explorer 157
Refreshments	The Barge Inn (01672 851222) and Honeystreet Mill Café (01672 851853) at Honeystreet; The Kings Arms (01380 860328) off route at All Cannings
Public transport	Buses between Devizes and Pewsey stop at Alton Priors (excluding Sundays)

This fairly long walk starts by crossing over Walker's Hill, with a great view across the Vale of Pewsey, and then drops down through the neighbouring villages of Alton Barnes and Alton Priors. From Honeystreet the walk follows the peaceful Kennet and Avon Canal before rising back onto the chalk downs, crossing over Tan Hill. The final part follows the ancient Wansdyke before skirting round Milk Hill – the highest point in Wiltshire – and passing the Alton Barnes White Horse.

From the car park cross over the road, go through a gate and immediately left through another gate. Follow the permissive path southwards through the field. Go through a gate on the right and bear half-left (south-west) up Walker's Hill, passing through a gate on the way to reach a col (SU 111 635) just to the right of **Adam's Grave**, a Neolithic long barrow or burial mound.

> From the top of the hill there is a lovely **view**, including south across the Vale of Pewsey to Salisbury Plain and east following the convoluted chalk ridge past Knap Hill (Walk 22), crowned by the earthworks of a Neolithic causewayed camp dating from around 3500BC.

The view east to Knap Hill (Walk 22) from Adam's Grave

Alternatively, 400m from the col turn left over the ridge (open access land) down to a gate. Go through, turn right and go through another gate, then follow the road downhill for 75m (care required).

After admiring the view follow a good path southwards (slope down to the right; Adam's Grave to the left) from the col down to a gate. Do not go through but stay in the field and turn left (White Horse Trail), parallel with road on right for 325m to a gate. Turn sharp right through the gate and shortly go through another gate, then walk down the road for 75m (care required). ◄ Then go left across the road and through a field entrance.

Follow the tree-shaded bridleway (Ridge Way) downhill. Continue past a house to join a lane in **Alton Priors**. Go left and then right at the junction past an old thatched barn to the lane end. Go through the turnstile and head across the field, keeping right of the All Saints Church to the trees (to visit the church go left at the path junction).

Inside the Norman **All Saints Church**, cared for by the Churches

134

Conservation Trust, are some fine Jacobean carved wooden choir stalls, a tomb chest to William Button (d.1590) and two sarsen stones hidden under trapdoors in the floor. Maybe these are from an earlier sacred site – early Christian churches were sometimes built on existing religious sites. Outside in the churchyard stands an ancient yew tree (another pagan symbol) said to be well over 1000 years old.

Keep to the cobbled path through two turnstiles and across footbridges to reach a path junction in the middle of the next field.
▶ Turn left and leave through a gate

To miss out the church go straight on to another turnstile onto the road and turn right.

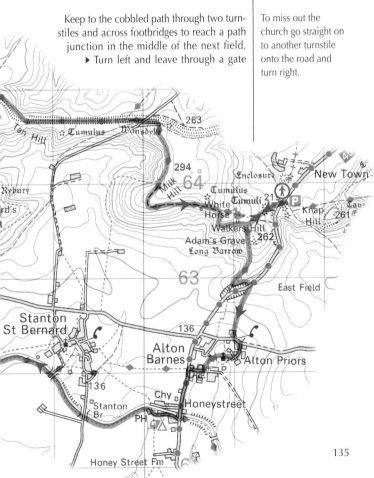

135

with the Church of St Mary the Virgin on the left; turn right along the lane through **Alton Barnes**.

The **Church of St Mary the Virgin** dates back to Saxon times. Call in to see the 16th-century tie-beamed and wind-braced roof, a Georgian gallery and some interesting monuments.

After 200m a field entrance on the right gives access to a memorial on the last remaining air-raid shelter (SU 104 617) from the Second World War.

At the T-junction turn left along the road towards **Honeystreet**. ◄ Cross the **Kennet and Avon Canal** and immediately turn right to join the towpath (50m before the bridge, along the track on the right is the Honeystreet Mill Café).

The **Kennet and Avon Canal**, which opened in 1810, provided a transport link between Bristol and the River Thames at Reading until the development of much faster railway links brought about its gradual decline. Fortunately, after years of neglect the canal has now been fully restored.

The track to the left leads to All Cannings – The Kings Arms pub is 800m each way; the 13th-century All Saints Church is 200m further on.

Follow the towpath westwards for 3.5km, passing The Barge Inn after 300m, to reach the fourth bridge (number 128) across the canal. ◄ Turn right over the bridge and immediately fork right, following the grassy strip across the field towards the buildings. Continue along the track, cross over the road and keep ahead uphill to two gates side by side. Go through the left-hand gate and follow the enclosed bridleway for 175m. Keep ahead across the field to leave through a gate. Continue uphill passing through a gate on the way to another gate near the top. From here admire the view, which includes the earthworks of Rybury Iron Age hill fort just to the south.

The walk joins the Mid Wilts Way, White Horse Trail and Wansdyke Path here.

Continue through the gate and follow the left-hand fence over **Tan Hill** to reach the **Wansdyke**. ◄

The **Wansdyke**, a massive linear earthwork dating from Saxon times (late fifth century), stretches east across the Marlborough Downs above the Vale of Pewsey from Morgan's Hill (Walk 20) to

*The linear earthwork
of the Wansdyke
stretches out across
Tan Hill*

Marlborough. The earthwork is probably named after the Saxon god Woden; hence it became 'Woden's Dyke' and, eventually, Wansdyke. The earthwork may have been built as a defensive structure to stop West Saxons encroaching from the upper Thames Valley, or maybe its purpose was one of demarking territorial areas; opinion is divided.

Turn right and follow the impressive earthwork for 2km as it sweeps along the downs. Exit through a gate and turn left on the track, then immediately fork right uphill for 200m, still heading east. Turn right through a gate to enter Pewsey Downs National Nature Reserve (NNR) (information board); the walk continues to follow the White Horse Trail and Mid Wilts Way (the Wansdyke Path goes straight on).

The final part of the walk contours round Walkers Hill – here looking back to the Alton Barnes White Horse

The **Pewsey Downs NNR** consists of a large expanse of chalk grassland on the steep south-facing slope. Plants include Common spotted, Frog and Fragrant orchids; butterflies include Marble white and Chalkhill blue.

Head across the field, go through a gate and follow the fence line on the left as it contours south and then curves right and left round **Milk Hill**. At 294m this is the highest point in Wiltshire and Britain's second highest chalk hill after Walbury Hill (Walk 26). Continue eastwards, pass through a gate and keep ahead, passing just above the **Alton Barnes White Horse**; the horse was commissioned by Robert Pile in 1812. Follow the level path as it contours round Walker's Hill to reach the col just west of Adam's Grave (SU 111 635), passed earlier in the walk. From here, head north-east retracing the route back down to the car park.

WALK 22

Knap Hill and Oare

Start/finish	Car park near Knap Hill, 1.9km north of Alton Barnes (SU 115 638); public transport start (bus): White Hart stop in Oare on the A345 (SU 158 631)
Distance	11.3km (7 miles) or (via Gopher Wood) 6.4km (4 miles)
Ascent	270m or 130m
Time	3½hr or 2hr
Map	OS Explorer 157
Refreshments	None (nearby pub and café at Honeystreet – see Walk 21)
Public transport	Bus services between Swindon and Salisbury stop at Oare

This walk heads north-east past Golden Ball Hill to reach Gopher Wood and then follows the Mid Wilts Way/White Horse Trail over Huish Hill before descending to Oare. The return route meanders past Draycott Fitz Payne and then climbs back towards Gopher Wood. The final section follows the crest of the downs westwards, with the option to visit the top of Knap Hill for great views. A shorter walk missing out Oare is also described.

From the end of the car park follow the track south-eastwards for 150m and turn left through a gate. Follow the fence on the left for a while, and then continue straight on below and left of **Knap Hill** to reach two gates side by side. Go through the left-hand gate and follow the fence line on the right, heading north-east gently uphill to cross an **earthwork** (SU 124 640). Continue north-eastwards across the open grass field as the fence falls away to the right, aiming for the trees. Cross a stile just left of the trees and pond; the walk now follows the right-hand boundary for 800m.

At the far-right corner go through a gate and continue through the next field, following the fence on the right. At the field corner continue along the narrow path beside

The route skirts to the left of Knap Hill

Just to the north are the earthworks of the former medieval village of Shaw.

the trees (left) and then follow the right-hand boundary as it bears right to head south-east. ◀

Pass the dip and keep ahead between fences going gently uphill. Pass over the brow and continue south-eastwards down across the field to a gate and track. Bear right along the track through the trees to a path and bridleway junction; the walk turns left here. Straight ahead is a track (path) that heads down-hill; half-right is a bridleway into Gopher Wood; and to the right, through a gate, is the route of the optional short-cut.

Short-cut via Gopher Wood

Turn right through the gate and head gently uphill. Cross a stile beside a gate and keep ahead to cross another stile beside Gopher Wood. Head diagonally left to a fingerpost and turn right to rejoin the main walk (this point is indicated in the sidebar on page 142).

For the main walk go through a gate and follow the grassy track gently uphill, heading eastwards (Mid Wilts Way/ White Horse Trail), with a line of hawthorn bushes on the right.

The 109km (68 mile) **Mid Wilts Way** meanders through Wiltshire from Ham, near the eastern border with Berkshire, to Mere, close to Wiltshire's western boundary with Dorset. The **White Horse Trail** visits all eight white-horse hill figures within Wiltshire, seven of which are within the North Wessex Downs (145km/90 miles).

Go through a gate in the top-left corner and immediately turn right through another gate. Follow the fence on the right along two sides of the field (views of Pewsey Vale over to the right). Go through a gate and continue straight on (White Horse Trail) through the field to a gate in the hedge on **Huish Hill** (80m left of the right-hand field corner). Follow the enclosed bridleway (to the right

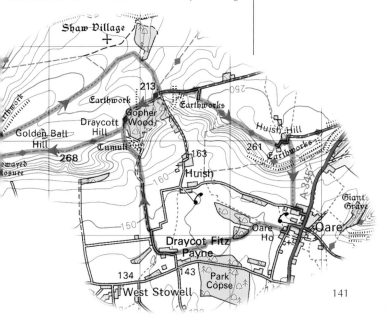

of a track) in the same direction, bear left along the gravel track and follow it to the right, then as it swings left, turn right along the enclosed path.

Go through a gate at the end and continue straight on downhill with the fence on the left. Stop at the seat to admire the views and then continue steeply down towards **Oare**. Go through a gate (Mid Wilts Trail) and follow the field edge straight on to a lane. Turn left along this, passing a school to reach the **A345**.

Turn right down the pavement for 150m, passing the bus stop. ◀ Turn right along Rudge Lane, following it as it curves left. Just before Oare House turn right and follow the bridleway past the buildings (not the path that forks right), cross the stile and follow the left-hand field boundary to the corner. Turn left through a gate and head south-west across the field (fritillaries flower here in spring), crossing the avenue of trees to a copse.

> Look left to see the large Georgian-styled **Oare House**, while to the right is a rather modern addition. The unusual steel-and-glass pagoda-styled garden house at the end of the avenue of trees was designed by IM Pei, who also designed the glass pyramid at the Louvre in Paris.

Follow the left edge of the wood, and then continue across the field following the line of mature trees. Go through a gate and turn left for 25m before turning right and following the field margin on the right. Leave through a gate and continue along the lane through **Draycot Fitz Payne**. Follow the lane as it turns right, and at the next right-hand bend fork left (straight on), following a track along the right-hand field margin. Go through a gate (open access land) and keep ahead uphill. At the split fork left, skirting round the spur crowned with tumuli, and go through a gate at the top to reach a fingerpost on **Draycott Hill**. ◀

Turn left and follow the Mid Wilts Way westwards along the ridge, with the fence on the left. After crossing a stile continue with the fence on right. Cross another stile

If using public transport (bus) you start the walk here.

The shorter walk rejoins here.

and continue along the crest of **Golden Ball Hill** before gently descending to the two side-by-side gates passed earlier.

Once through the gate either head directly back to the car park or, for a great view, bear slightly left over the top of **Knap Hill** (open access land) before heading down to the car park (this adds 200m).

Heading back past Knap Hill – take a short detour to the top to admire the view

The summit of **Knap Hill** is crowned by the earthworks of a Neolithic causewayed enclosure dating from 3500BC. The view looks south across the Vale of Pewsey to Salisbury Plain, and nearby are the twin tops of Woodborough Hill and Picked Hill; to the west is Walker's Hill, Adam's Grave and Milk Hill (Walk 21); while to the east are views along the scarp past Huish Hill, Giant's Grave and Martinsell Hill (Walk 23).

WALK 23

Martinsell Hill and Wootton Rivers

Start/finish	Car park at Martinsell Hill (SU 183 645)
Alternative start/ finish	Pewsey rail station (SU 160 604)
Distance	13km (8 miles) or (start/finish at Pewsey station) 15km (9¼ miles)
Ascent	230m or 265m
Time	3¾hr or 4¼hr
Map	OS Explorer 157
Refreshments	The Royal Oak (01672 810322) at Wootton Rivers; The Waterfront (01672 564020) at Pewsey (off route)
Public transport	Trains to Pewsey; bus service to Pewsey from Swindon and Salisbury

This lovely walk sets out along the crest of the downs, skirts round Martinsell Hill and passes the Giant's Grave, with magnificent views across the Vale of Pewsey, before heading down to the Kennet and Avon Canal. A level walk along the canal towpath leads to the village of Wootton Rivers, with its thatched pub. The final section climbs back up to the downs and follows Mud Lane back to the start.

Alternative start from Pewsey station
Leave from platform 2, head down the access road, cross over the main road (A345) and turn right for a few metres. Fork left along the surfaced path (Way's Way) through the trees. Continue along the surfaced drive to pass to the right of the Buckleaze Mill, with the railway on right. Continue along the surfaced path, and at the split keep left along the path, with houses on the left. Keep ahead along the lane to the right-hand bend and turn left. Follow the tree-shaded bridleway to the canal bridge and turn right to join the main walk (SU 164 611) (this point is indicated in the sidebar on page 146).

At the car park stand with your back to road and head west-south-west through the gate and follow the Mid Wilts Way alongside the right-hand fence. Where the trees (and fence) fall away to the right bear left (south) up between trees on **Martinsell Hill**. Continue along the crest of the slope and pass more trees. Go through a gate and head south-west past a seat with a great view across the Vale of Pewsey. Follow the fence on the left (trees on right) and then continue through the field, still with the fence on left. Ignore a gate on the left and keep to the permissive path along the field edge to the far corner. Keep ahead through a gate and follow the fence on the right through another gate, soon passing through the earthworks of **Giant's Grave** to reach a trig point. ▶

Having admired the views, head steeply downhill following the fence on the right, go through a gate in the bottom-right corner and continue straight on (south-south-east) across the field. Go straight over the cross track (400m to the right is Oare, with bus connections – see Walk 22) and follow the path along the right-hand field margin.

The earthworks are the remains of an Iron Age promontory hill fort or settlement, protected on its eastern edge by a rampart and ditch. The route is now following the Mid Wilts Way and White Horse Trail.

Heading down past the Giant's Grave on Martinsell Hill

The route starting from the rail station in Pewsey joins here and follows the canal north-eastwards to Wootton Rivers.

Turn left along the lane for 200m and then turn right (south) along the track (bridleway) to the bridge (Pains Bridge) over the **Kennet and Avon Canal** (SU 164 611). ◄ About 700m to the west along the towpath (canal on right)is Pewsey Wharf (pay and display parking, and The Waterfront pub).

Cross the bridge and immediately turn sharp left to the canal and then turn right (north-east, canal on left) along the canal towpath for 4km (passing four bridges) to reach the lock and bridge at **Wootton Rivers**. The canal opened in 1810, while the railway running parallel with the canal opened in 1862 and now forms the line passing through Reading and Westbury.

> **Wootton Rivers**, first recorded in AD804, gained part of its name from the de la Riviere family, who held the manor from the early 13th century. In 1441 the manor was sold to Sir John Seymour of Savernake and then passed through a succession of Seymours and Dukes of Somerset until 1692, when it was bequeathed to St John's College, Cambridge.
>
> The small 14th-century St Andrew's Church has a picturesque wooden steeple and a clock made by local man, John Spratt, to commemorate George V's coronation in 1911. The clock was made from scrap metal, and on the face the numbers have been replaced with the words 'Glory be to God'; he also made a clock for the Wesleyan Chapel (now a private house), but on that one the words were 'To God be glory'.

Leave the canal here and turn left along the road through the village, passing St Andrew's Church (left) and then

the thatch-roofed Royal Oak (right). ▶ Keep ahead for 250m and shortly after passing the former Wesleyan Chapel (right), fork left along a track with houses on the right at first. Continue uphill to enter a field.

The walk now follows the Mid Wilts Way for 3.6km (2¼ miles) from Wootton Rivers back to the start.

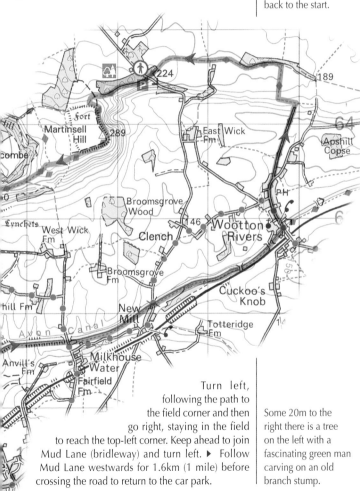

Turn left, following the path to the field corner and then go right, staying in the field to reach the top-left corner. Keep ahead to join Mud Lane (bridleway) and turn left. ▶ Follow Mud Lane westwards for 1.6km (1 mile) before crossing the road to return to the car park.

Some 20m to the right there is a tree on the left with a fascinating green man carving on an old branch stump.

WALK 24
Great Bedwyn and Wilton

Start/finish	Great Bedwyn rail station (SU 279 645); on-street parking in village or beside the canal (SU 280 644)
Distance	11.4km (7 miles) or (shorter route) 8.5km (5¼ miles)
Ascent	200m or 160m
Time	3¼hr or 2½hr
Map	OS Explorer 157
Refreshments	The Three Tuns (01672 870280) and shop at Great Bedwyn; café at Crofton Pumping Station (01672 870300); The Swan (01672 870274) at Wilton
Public transport	Trains to Great Bedwyn; bus links to Marlborough and Hungerford (excluding Sundays)

From Great Bedwyn, known as 'Bedewinde' in the Domesday Book, the walk meanders alongside the Kennet and Avon Canal and then through Wilton Brail to reach the famous Crofton Pumping Station. The return passes picturesque Wilton Windmill before heading through the wooded landscape of Bedwyn Brail to arrive back at Great Bedwyn. A shorter version of the walk is also described.

The canal opened in 1810, followed by the opening of the railway between Reading and Westbury in 1862.

From the rail station in **Great Bedwyn** head south-west to the main road (Brook Street) and turn left. After crossing the **Kennet and Avon Canal** turn right and head through the car park to join the towpath. ◄

Follow the towpath south-westwards for 900m, and after the second **bridge** (Mill Bridge) turn left through a gate and small parking area. Follow the lane south-east-wards for 250m, and where it swings right (**Brail Farm**) turn hard right on a track through the trees. Once in the field bear left along the left-hand margin gently uphill. Pass a small communication mast and continue alongside the wood, heading gently downhill for 300m to a cross-junction.

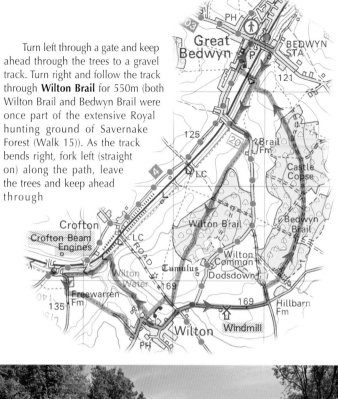

Turn left through a gate and keep ahead through the trees to a gravel track. Turn right and follow the track through **Wilton Brail** for 550m (both Wilton Brail and Bedwyn Brail were once part of the extensive Royal hunting ground of Savernake Forest (Walk 15)). As the track bends right, fork left (straight on) along the path, leave the trees and keep ahead through

The route through Wilton Brail

This track was once a Roman road that ran between Venta Bulgarum (Winchester) and Cunetio (near Mildenhall, Walk 14).

two fields separated by a hedge. At the far side descend through trees to a track and turn right uphill for 75m before turning left up the bank (signposted for Wilton Wide Water and The Swan). ◄ Continue across the field down towards **Wilton**.

At the field corner, stay in the field and turn right – signposted to the beam engines, now following the Mid Wilts Way.

Shorter route

Exit the field and turn left along the lane to reach The Swan in Wilton and rejoin the main route (this point is indicated in the sidebar on page 151).

For the main walk follow the left-hand field edge, later with **Wilton Water** on the left. At the end of the lake, cross over the sluice gate to rejoin the canal towpath and turn left (west) past the lock, with the railway and Crofton Pumping Station over to the right. To visit the Pumping Station cross the canal via the lock gate and follow the path through the tunnel, under the railway and then up the steps. Retrace the route back to the canal towpath and turn right.

> Located near the summit of the canal, beside Wilton Water, is the world-famous **Crofton Pumping Station**. Built in 1807, the pumps were used to raise water 12m from natural springs at Wilton up to the summit of the canal to replenish the water lost each time a boat went through a lock. In response to increasing traffic along the canal, Wilton Water was created in 1836 to provide a larger store of water that could be pumped into the canal. Although electric pumps have been installed, the original magnificent Cornish Beam engines – the oldest working steam engines in the world – are still used on several occasions throughout the year (01672 870300).

Crofton Pump House on the Kennet and Avon Canal

Leave the canal at the next bridge and turn left along the road to a junction. Fork left (signposted to Grafton) and follow the road, which quickly curves right past **Freewarren Farm**. Some 175m after the farm entrance turn left up the bank (footpath sign), cross the stile and follow the left-hand boundary through two fields separated by two stiles. Cross the stile in the far-left corner of the second field, go through the trees, and cross a footbridge. Continue alongside the left-hand trees and then along the track to a minor road.

Turn left downhill towards Wilton and follow road as it curves right, passing the pond, to a junction beside The Swan. ▶ Keep left, following the road uphill, and go straight on at the next junction. At the split, fork right towards Shallbourne; after 400m there is an access track on the right for the **windmill** and picnic area.

The shorter route rejoins the main route here.

Wilton Windmill, the only working windmill within the North Wessex Downs, was built in 1821. After standing derelict for 50 years, the mill has been lovingly restored to full working condition. Built from brick, the mill has a fantail that keeps the sails aligned with the wind, acting as an automatic rudder (01672 608691).

Continue straight on along the road to the next junction (right) and turn left along the track for 200m. Go right along a path through the trees and bear right (signposted Great Bedwyn) to a crossing gravel track. Turn left and follow the track (bridleway) through **Bedwyn Brail**.

After 800m continue through a large clearing and pass just left of a wooden barn before continuing northwards along the track. Keep ahead at the next junction, and on reaching a grassy area surrounded by trees, fork left. Continue through trees to enter a field.

Follow the left-hand edge, ignore the path to the left, and drop down through the next field to a gate slightly right of the corner. Go through the gate, straight over the bridge crossing the canal, and with great care go through gates either side of the **railway**. Keep ahead through the field and alongside the churchyard wall, with the Church of St Mary the Virgin to the right.

The **Church of St Mary the Virgin** dates from 1092, although most of what is visible dates from the 12th and 13th centuries. Inside the rather large church is an impressive monument to Sir John Seymour, father of Jane Seymour, who married Henry VIII in 1536, becoming his third wife; their son became Edward VI. The church also holds the stone figure of a knight, believed to be Sir Adam de Stokke (d.1313), and the tomb of Sir Roger de Stokke (d.1333), son of Sir Adam.

On the wall of the post office are some works by Lloyd's stonemason's yard (est 1790, closed 2009).

Go through a gate and turn right along the road through Great Bedwyn to a junction (200m to the left is The Three Tuns pub). ◀ Turn right downhill and then left back to the rail station.

NORTH HAMPSHIRE DOWNS

Walk 27 heading towards Pilot Hill, highest point in Hampshire

WALK 25
Tidcombe and Hippenscombe Bottom

Start/finish	St Michael's Church at Tidcombe (SU 290 582), 3km south-east off the A338 at SU 280 606; limited roadside parking
Distance	9.7km (6 miles)
Ascent	220m
Time	2¾hr
Map	OS Explorer 131
Refreshments	None (nearby pubs at Lower Chute, Vernham Dean, Wilton)
Public transport	None

This short but hilly walk, situated close to the Wiltshire–Hampshire border, offers some great views across the rolling North Hampshire Downs. From the Wiltshire hamlet of Tidcombe the walk heads up over Tidcombe Down to cross the Chute Causeway – a former Roman road – and then follows tracks towards Haydown Hill. After a steep descent the walk gently meanders up along Hippenscombe Bottom before recrossing the Chute Causeway as it heads back to Tidcombe with views towards Salisbury Plain.

> **St Michael's Church** in Tidcombe mostly dates from the 14th century, with Victorian restorations. However, there may have been an earlier church here as the font is believed to be Saxon (probably dating from AD850). From the churchyard there is a good view of the mid 18th-century red-brick Tidcombe Manor.

With St Michael's Church behind you turn right up the lane, and after passing house number 11 (but before the lane curves right to pass the last house) fork left (south) down the waymarked path. Cross a stile and continue through the field, passing just left of a fenced pond. Bear slightly left at the copse, keeping the fenced trees on the right, and then continue up the grassy slope. Pass the corner of a wood and continue uphill. Take a rest and admire the view from here – nearby and to the north-north-west are Wilton Windmill and Crofton Pumping Station (Walk 24), with the Marlborough Downs in the distance.

Continue more gently up through the field; over to the right are the earthworks of a Neolithic long barrow (3400–2400BC). Leave the field over a stile beside a gate and cross over the minor road known as the **Chute Causeway**. ▶

Take the track opposite (bridleway); the walk now follows this track for 1.8km to reach a track junction at SU 308 568. At first there are beech trees on the right, with a view to the left out across Maccombe Down, with its ancient linear earthwork. Keep ahead past a belt of trees, then pass **Down Barn** (and water tank) over to your right, surrounded by trees, and gradually descend to the

This follows part of a former Roman road that ran between Venta Bulgarum (Winchester) and Cunetio (near Mildenhall, Walk 14).

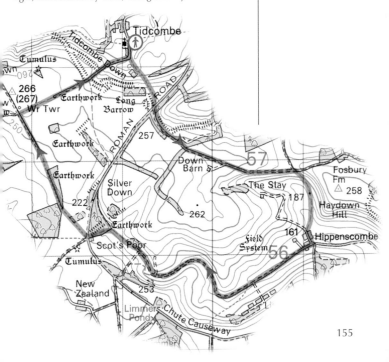

Following the track up along Hippenscombe Bottom – keep right at the trees

junction, with **Haydown Hill** ahead. Distant views stretch eastwards over the North Hampshire Downs, taking in the communication mast on Cottington's Hill near Hannington (Walk 30), 22km to the east.

Turn right down the bridleway towards **Hippenscombe**. Pass between the farm buildings to a T-junction and turn right. The route now follows the track along the sinuous valley of Hippenscombe Bottom for 2.5km and, where the track turns left uphill, go straight on, still following the bridleway along the valley (fence on left).

After 200m go through a gate and continue between bushes (left) and a fence (right). Then fork left following the left-hand edge of Scotspoor Plantation up to a thatched cottage (left) at **Scot's Poor**.

Recross the Chute Causeway (minor road) to enter a field (ignore the track junction over to the left). Bear diagonally right (north-west) across the field, passing just left of a stand of trees, and then continue along the right-hand

margin. Continue through the trees of Scotspoor Wood, passing a gate, and follow the track north-westwards, with Picked Plantation on the right, to reach a track junction just before a **water tower**; to the left is a distant view towards Salisbury Plain.

Turn right through the gate and head north-eastwards through the field, passing just right of a copse. Go through a gate and continue along the track between fields and start descending; from here there is a great view to the east-north-east that includes Walbury Hill (Walk 26). At the track junction on **Tidcombe Down** – notice the ancient earthwork on the right – keep ahead steeply down the tarmac track back to **Tidcombe**.

The final section down to Tidcombe offers a great view of the North Hampshire Downs

WALK 26
Inkpen and Walbury Hill

Start/finish	Recreation ground car park on Post Office Road in Inkpen (SU 372 641), 5km south from the A4 via Kintbury. Alternative parking/start: Walbury Hill (SU 370 620 or SU 379 616)
Distance	10.8km (6¾ miles)
Ascent	245m
Time	3¼hr
Map	OS Explorer 158
Refreshments	The Crown and Garter (01488 668325) at Inkpen Common
Public transport	Buses between Newbury and Hungerford stop at Inkpen (excluding Sundays)

From Inkpen, home to Britain's largest display of wild purple crocuses in spring, the route passes through Lower Green before heading south for a steep climb up Inkpen Hill. The walk then heads east along the crest of the downs, passing the stark outline of Combe Gibbet and offering some great views before passing over Walbury Hill, the highest chalk hill in England. The route then leaves these lofty heights to pass through Inkpen Common back to the start.

From the car park turn right along Post Office Road for 40m and then right along Pottery Lane (byway). After 200m, on the left just before The Old Forge (private house), is a hedge-lined track that gives access to BBOWT's Crocus Field Nature Reserve.

The **Crocus Field Nature Reserve** is home to thousands of purple spring crocuses (*Crocus vernus*) that flower here in late February and March, forming Britain's largest display of wild spring crocuses. The plants have been here for several centuries, and some suggest that they were brought back by the Knights Templar during the Crusades.

Continue along the lane as it starts to descend and curve right, and after the last house on the left, go left through a gate. Follow the enclosed path, go through gates either side of a small field and continue across the larger field towards **Manor Farm**. Leave through a gate, cross the minor road and follow the enclosed path ahead (buildings on the left) to its end. Turn left, soon following a raised wooden walkway, then cross a footbridge. Keep ahead along the enclosed path, then a driveway, to a minor road at **Lower Green**.

Turn left and keep right at the junction, following the road signposted for Ham and Shalbourne. After passing West Court house fork left on the track (driveway) past the end of the cottage. Cross the stile and bear left

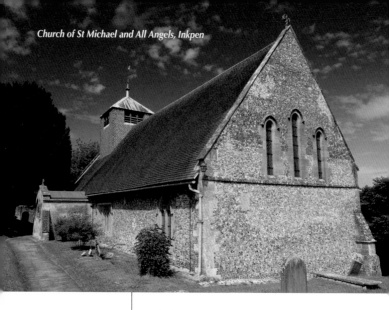

Church of St Michael and All Angels, Inkpen

To visit the church turn left and then right up through the lychgate.

(south) through the field to a stile by some trees. Continue through the next field, cross a stile to join a minor road near the Church of St Michael and All Angels and turn right. ◀

The **Church of St Michael and All Angels** was probably founded by Sir Roger de Ingpen, a Knight Templar, in 1220; his effigy can be seen in the chancel on the north side of the altar. The church also has an oak rood screen, complete with large foliated cross (or rood), and five 20th-century religious wall paintings. Overlooking the church is the late 17th-century Inkpen House (or Old Rectory).

Follow the road down to a T-junction, go left towards Ham and Shalbourne for 200m, and turn left along the signposted track (bridleway). Go through a gate and follow the left-hand field edge for 100m before bearing right alongside the hedge and trees on the right. Continue between fields and then straight on at the junction, following the scrub-lined bridleway – Bungum

Lane. At the end, go through a gate and head diagonally left (south-east) steeply up **Inkpen Hill**, admiring the view on the way. Later bear right over the brow of the hill towards the bushes. At the path junction go right, then quickly fork left through gates to join a track and turn left for 600m to reach **Combe Gibbet**. The view extends north over the Kennet Valley to the Berkshire Downs, north-east to the distant Chilterns, and south-east over the North Hampshire Downs.

> **Combe Gibbet** was built in 1676 to hang a local man and his mistress close to the spot where they murdered his wife and son; although never used again, the gibbet has been replaced several times. The story of the murders was used as the basis of the 1948 film 'The Black Legend', produced by a group of Oxford undergraduates including John Schlesinger, who later became a well-known film director.
>
> The gibbet also marks the start, or end, of two of Hampshire's long-distance paths – the 114km (71 mile) Wayfarer's Walk, which heads to the coast near Portsmouth, and the 73km (45 mile) Test Way, which follows the Test Valley to Southampton Water.

After admiring the view, continue eastwards down the track. Cross over the minor road, head for the car park (an alternative parking/start point) and take the track on the right-hand side.

> On the north side of the road, opposite the car park, is a **memorial stone**. This stone commemorates the 9th Battalion, the Parachute Regiment, who trained here in 1944 prior to their successful assault on the German coastal artillery battery at Merville, France.

Follow the track east-south-east, passing to the right of the car park, and continue over **Walbury Hill**.

Heading down across West Woodhay Down

At 297m **Walbury Hill** is the highest chalk hill in England and the highest point in Berkshire. It is crowned by Berkshire's largest Iron Age hill fort.

Pass another car park (alternative parking/start point), cross over the minor road and go through a gate into a field. Follow the signposted bridleway diagonally east-north-east down across **West Woodhay Down**, passing just below a small wood. Keep ahead (east-north-east), along the contour of the hill aiming at the bottom of another small wood. Go through a gate and turn left down the minor road for 300m to a crossing track. Turn left along the track (bridleway), which soon swings right towards **Highwood Farm**.

At the field corner, beside the farm buildings, stay in the field and turn left (north-west), following a track alongside the right-hand field margin. Follow this as it swings left, with a wood on the right. At the western field corner follow the track to the right (keeping the trees on

Once back below the downs the walk follows field edges, here with a view of West Woodhay house

the right), and then continue along the field margin to a minor road beside **Park House**. ▶ Bear right (straight on), heading north-eastwards along the road for 450m, and once level with the buildings (right) turn left along the tarmac track (restricted byway). Continue past some houses and follow the track straight on past Prosser's Farm to a minor road beside The Crown and Garter at **Inkpen Common**.

Cross over the road and follow the track opposite. After passing a cottage bear left and continue westwards along the restricted byway through the trees for 400m. Keep ahead along the track, past a cottage, and then turn right through a gate (footpath sign). Head north-west along the fenced path, go through a gate to a road in **Inkpen** and turn right for 50m back to the start on the left.

On the way, look right to see West Woodhay House.

WALK 27
Ashmansworth and Faccombe

Start/finish	Village green and war memorial in Ashmansworth, 1.3km west from the A343 (SU 415 574); limited roadside parking
Distance	9.5km (6 miles)
Ascent	280m
Time	3hr
Map	OS Explorer 131
Refreshments	The Jack Russell Inn (01264 737315) at Faccombe
Public transport	Limited bus service to Ashmansworth (better service to Three Legged Cross/A343 (SU 430 575) beside Three Legs House, 1.1km off route via Wayfarer's Walk footpath) from Andover and Newbury (excluding Sundays)

This half-day walk explores the beautiful North Hampshire Downs in the far north-west corner of Hampshire. From picturesque Ashmansworth the walk heads through open fields and woods to visit Faccombe, home to a pub and church. The walk continues north, climbing up Pilot Hill – the highest point in Hampshire. It's the ideal place to take a rest and admire the stunning views before following part of the Wayfarer's Walk on the way back to Ashmansworth.

Ashmansworth, Hampshire's highest village, lying at 235m, has a lovely collection of thatched cottages, including the 'chocolate-box' Mere Cottage overlooking the village green and war memorial. The village, known as Esmereswarde (meaning 'ash pool') in the 12th century, was first mentioned in a Saxon charter in AD909, although Roman artefacts have been found locally, suggesting a much longer history. For several hundred years the manor was held by Winchester Abbey before being acquired by the present owners, the Earls of Carnarvon (Highclere Castle), in the 19th century. The English composer Gerald Finzi lived in the village for a number of years.

From the triangular village green (war memorial), where the road splits, take the right-hand road signposted to Faccombe, heading south-west for 500m; take care as the lane is narrow in places. Just after a sharp right-hand bend the road curves left. Go straight on past a gate and head north-west down through the field, soon with trees on the right.

At the bottom of the slope, keep ahead up a short rise and continue straight on following a narrow path up through the trees. Once back in an open field continue (northwards) up to the trees. Turn left (west) following the edge of **Privet Copse** (right) for 150m to a junction with a wide grassy strip on the right (north) between

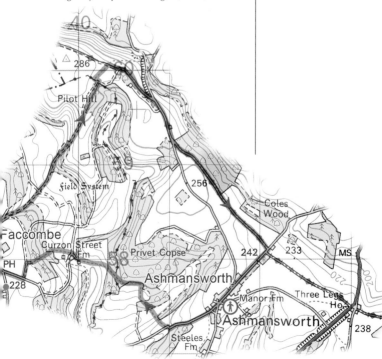

two woods, an open field on the left, and a track heading north-west between the two. Take this track down through the trees of Robins Croft Copse for 300m to a junction.

Turn left (west) downhill, with a large field on the left and soon trees on the right. Later the track curves right to a signposted junction with a brick barn on the left at **Curzon Street Farm**. Take the second left (west) uphill, passing to the right of another building, and shortly before the field corner fork slightly left and continue steeply up through the trees (crossing a track on the way). At the top bear left along the right-hand field edge. Pass a gate, turn right along the lane to a junction, and turn right towards **Faccombe**. Follow the main street through the village, ignoring all side roads to the left; some 50m to the left, at the first junction, is the village pond and The Jack Russell Inn. Keep ahead past the early 18th-century Faccombe Manor (right) and then the Church of St Barnabas (left).

Church of St Barnabas in Faccombe

For many years the main village in the area was Netherton; however, within the last 200 years the population has drifted up to **Faccombe**. The Church of St Barnabas, built in the second half of the 19th century, contains a decorated Norman font and several 17th-century memorials that originated from Netherton's 13th-century church.

Before the last building on the right, fork right along a tarmac track (footpath sign), and then fork left along a track following the Brenda Parker Way. ▶ Keep left (straight on) at the first split, and after 20m fork right at the second, following the track downhill, with the field on the left, views ahead and Roe Wood to the right. Keep ahead at a crossing track, now with a hedge on the left and field to the right, and then continue up through the trees; this is quite a steep climb up the side of **Pilot Hill** – the highest point in Hampshire at 286m.

Keep to the track, later following trees on the right. Drop down to a dip and then go up to a right-hand bend. Here, go left over a stile, follow the right-hand

The view to the north from the crest of the North Hampshire Downs

This 126km (78-mile) route, developed by the North Hampshire Ramblers Group, runs between Andover and Aldershot.

Mere Cottage in Ashmansworth – a typical 'chocolate-box' thatched cottage on the village green

For bus connections at Three Legged Cross/A343 continue along the Wayfarer's Walk for 1.1km.

field edge and cross another stile. Bear right through the scrub and continue slightly right (north-eastwards) across the field to a crossing bridleway – soon a great view opens out ahead, looking north across the Kennet Valley to the distant Lambourn Downs.

Turn right along the bridleway, following the Wayfarer's Walk (a 114km/71 mile route from Combe Gibbet to the coast near Portsmouth). Shortly dogleg left through the trees and continue along the track, passing a house (Charldown), down to a lane. Turn right up the lane, soon with views to the left through the trees. After 500m bear left along the Wayfarer's Walk (byway signpost) and follow the track south-eastwards for 1.6km along the edge of Bunkhanger Copse to a minor road. ◀ Turn right and head along the road back to **Ashmansworth**.

WALK 28

St Mary Bourne and the Bourne Valley

Start/finish	Recreation ground car park beside the village shop in Bourne Meadow, off the B3048 at St Mary Bourne (SU 421 503)
Distance	7.6km (4¾ miles)
Ascent	100m
Time	2hr
Map	OS Explorer 131
Refreshments	The George Inn (01264 318000) and shop at St Mary Bourne
Public transport	Bus service to Swampton/St Mary Bourne from Andover and Newbury (excluding Sundays)

This easy short walk explores the Bourne Valley, close to the southern edge of the North Wessex Downs. From picturesque St Mary Bourne the walk follows the Test Way past Swampton before climbing up Stoke Hill. Here it heads south-eastwards to join a lane that follows the course of a former Roman road before heading back down to St Mary Bourne.

From the car park head back to the main street (**B3048**) and turn left for 200m through the village to the war memorial.

> The picturesque village of **St Mary Bourne**, with its thatched cottages and historic St Peter's Church (see below), lies alongside the Bourne Rivulet – often just called 'The Bourne'. The stream, whose upper reaches are seasonal, is a tributary of the River Test, which it joins at Whitchurch. The author Harry Plunket Greene celebrated the Bourne Rivulet in his classic fly-fishing book *Where the Bright Waters Meet* (1924).

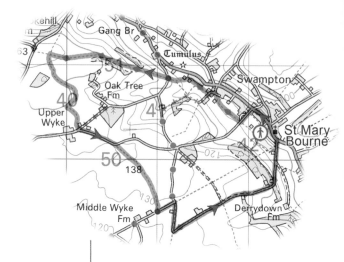

Turn left along the lane for 175m, and after passing Bourne House turn right through a gate; the walk now follows the Test Way and Brenda Parker Way for 2.4km. Head north-west through three fields separated by gates to arrive at a junction beside Haven Hill (left) in **Swampton**.

Take the second on the left – almost straight on – with the school on the right, and follow the main track as it swings left past some houses. After the last house on the right and before the track starts rising, turn right along an enclosed path (Test Way sign).

Ignore the crossing path, and at the end of the enclosed path turn left through a gate. Follow the right-hand field boundary up to a gate in the corner. Keep ahead through the trees into the field and turn right. Leave through a gate, cross the lane slightly right, go up some steps and continue, following the Test Way along the right-hand field boundary – which later bends left – for 250m.

At the marker post, dogleg right through the hedge into the adjacent field and continue, now following the left-hand field boundary. Go through the bushes at the field corner past a marker post and continue between the trees and fence for 600m, crossing four stiles. After the

fourth stile keep ahead into the field for a short way to a crossing path (SU 397 511) and turn left over the stile, leaving both the Test Way and Brenda Parker Way.

Continue through a gate and over a stile, either side of some trees, and then head diagonally south-south-east across the field to a stile 20m right of the field corner. Once in the next field follow the left-hand edge for a short distance and then head diagonally south-south-east across the field aiming for the trees. Turn left alongside the trees, before crossing a stile on the right, and follow a path through the trees to the right-hand side. Cross a stile into a paddock, turn left and cross two more stiles to join a lane near **Upper Wyke**. Bear left along the lane (not the track) for 400m, and at the left-hand bend turn right into the field. Follow the grassy strip, later a track, for 800m to a lane with **Middle Wyke Farm** to the right. ▶

Turn left along the lane, and where this goes left, turn right along a tree-lined path for 300m to a junction

Shortly after Middle Wyke Farm the walk rejoins the Test Way

The lane here follows the Portway, a former Roman road that ran between Sorviodunum (Old Sarum) and Calleva Atrebatum (Silchester).

The beautiful 12th-century Tournai marble font, St Peter's Church, St Mary Bourne

The walk now follows the Test Way back to the start.

with a hedge-lined track; turn left. ◄ Follow the track past some farm buildings (Lower Wyke Barn) and an open field, then keep ahead at a crossing path (wood on left). Shortly pass a cottage and follow the tarmac track past the entrance to **Derrydown House**. Continue down the lane to a T-junction and turn left along the B3048, soon passing some lovely thatched cottages and St Peter's Church (right).

> Step inside the 12th-century **St Peter's Church** to see the beautiful 12th-century Tournai marble font, one of only four in Hampshire (all were quarried and carved at Tournai in Belgium). The stained-glass windows include one in the north aisle given by the Bank of England – the window contains the figure of St Christopher surmounted by the 'Old Lady of Threadneedle Street'. Along the south wall is the rather worn effigy of Sir Roger des Andelys of Wyke Manor, who fought in the Crusades.

Follow the main street over the Bourne Rivulet (with The George Inn on the right), and fork left along Bourne Meadow back to the car park.

WALK 29

Ecchinswell and Ladle Hill

Start/finish	Village hall and recreation ground car park on the main street in Ecchinswell (SU 500 597). Alternative parking/ start: junction of Wayfarer's Walk and minor road, 3km south of Ecchinswell (SU 491 566)
Distance	13.6km (8½ miles)
Ascent	290m
Time	4hr
Map	OS Explorer 144
Refreshments	The Royal Oak (01635 297355) at Ecchinswell
Public transport	Limited bus service to Ecchinswell from Newbury (excluding Sundays)

From Ecchinswell this figure-of-eight walk takes a meandering route, gradually climbing to the top of Ladle Hill, which is crowned by the remains of an Iron Age fort and offers some great views. The walk then heads downhill, passing Sydmonton Court and then Nuthanger Farm, immortalised in Richard Adams's book *Watership Down*.

From the car park head west, away from the entrance, and follow the right-hand edge of the playing field. Continue straight on, following the trees along the right-hand side of the field, and then keep ahead through Crowmarsh Copse to reach a lane. Turn left up the lane, passing **Cowhouse Farm** to a junction. Cross straight over, following the track, which soon swings right and then left down past some cottages (right) to a track junction on the left at SU 485 587. ▶

This is the return route, so there is the option to shorten the walk here – turn left and follow the last section of the walk (distance: 6.3km/4miles).

Continue straight on along the track as it curves right to a split. Take the right-hand fork, with trees on the left and field on the right, to reach a minor road. Turn left past Wergs Manor and **Wergs Farm** to T-junction. Go straight across and keep ahead along the tree-shaded bridleway for 1.4km, later rising up through trees and scrub to an

From Ecchinswell the route heads through fields towards Cowhouse Farm

open field. Keep ahead along the grassy strip for 150m to a marker post at a junction with the Wayfarer's Walk. Turn left along the Wayfarer's Walk, still following a grassy strip and heading towards the top of Ladle Hill. At the fence turn right to walk alongside the fence on your left; soon a gate on the left gives access to **Ladle Hill** (open access land).

Ladle Hill is crowned by the remains of an unfinished Iron Age hill fort, while just to the north of the hill fort is a well-preserved disc barrow measuring 50m in diameter. Take time to admire the view. To the west and nearby is Beacon Hill, crowned by the remains of an Iron Age hill fort. (Buried on the hill is George Edward Stanhope Molyneux Herbert, fifth Earl of Carnarvon, who helped in the discovery of the tomb of Tutankhamen in the Valley of the Kings in 1922.) To the west-north-west Highclere Castle (home to the Earls of Carnarvon) might be visible; to the north is the Kennet Valley with the Berkshire Downs in the distance; and 40km to the north-east are the Chiltern Hills.

Continue eastwards along the grassy track, passing left of a tumulus (Bronze Age burial mound) to the field edge, and turn left for 125m. Turn right through a gate and follow the fence on the right. Pass some trees and bear right, keeping parallel with the fence. At the end, go through a gate and turn left down the track beside some large beech trees for 100m, and then turn left through a gate, passing an electricity pylon. ▶

The track straight on leads to a minor road with roadside parking (alternative parking/ start) (200m).

Follow the track downhill and continue between hedges towards **Sydmonton** passing four gates on the way. Turn left along the minor road for 175m. Turn right at the farm entrance and immediately fork right through a gate (barn on left). Continue straight on (north) for 700m to a track junction passed earlier; shortly after passing the last building on the left look hard right to catch sight of Sydmonton Court.

The **Sydmonton Court** estate – named after 'Sydeman', who appears in records in AD931, and 'tun', mean- ing 'farm' – was

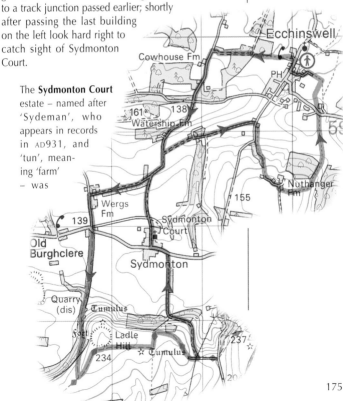

175

Heading down a good track towards Sydmonton

owned by Romsey Abbey until the Dissolution of the Monasteries in the 16th century. The estate was then granted to William Kingsmill and stayed in the family line for many generations. Sydmonton Court is now the country home of Lord Lloyd Webber of Sydmonton (aka Andrew Lloyd Webber); the church is private.

Bear right (straight on) and follow the track as it curves left to another junction passed earlier (SU 485 587). Turn right here following the open track. Keep ahead past the stable buildings at **Watership Farm**, go through a gate, and continue along the track to a minor road with a house opposite. Turn right, and within a few metres fork slightly left up the waymarked path, following the fence with trees on the right. Continue uphill and pass a small stable; keep ahead up the surfaced track to a house on the right and turn left. Keep to the right of a building and turn right up the track; to the left is Nuthanger Farm that played a part in Richard Adams's book *Watership Down* about the adventures of a group of rabbits.

After 30m turn left into the field and follow the left-hand margin as it later curves left. ▶ Continue downhill between Nuthanger Copse (left) and a fence (right). Keep ahead along the raised, tree-shaded path and then between hedges. Turn left along the minor road for 50m, and shortly after the driveway on the left (Clere House) turn right over a stile. Head north down across the field, passing a wooden electricity pole. Leave over a stile, cross the footbridge, and follow the left-hand field margin to a path junction. Turn left and follow the enclosed path, then keep ahead along the track as it curves left and right to become Mill Lane in **Ecchinswell**. At the T-junction (The Royal Oak is 150m to the left) turn right past the school and war memorial and then left back to the car park; 125m further along the road is St Lawrence's Church.

Recorded in the Domesday Book, **Ecchinswell** was held by Winchester Abbey for several hundred years. The late 19th-century St Lawrence's Church replaced an earlier building.

To the south is the broad grassland slope of Watership Down – Walk 30.

The final part of the walk heading back to Ecchinswell

WALK 30

Kingsclere and Hannington

Start/finish	Junction of Swan Street and Anchor Road in Kingsclere (SU 525 586); car park in Anchor Road. Alternative parking/start: White Hill car park (SU 515 564)
Distance	12.8km (8 miles) or (shorter route) 9.2km (5¾ miles)
Ascent	305m or 225m
Time	3¾hr or 2¾hr
Map	OS Explorer 144
Refreshments	Shop, café, The Crown (01635 299500) and the Bel & The Dragon (01635 299342) at Kingsclere; The Vine (01635 298525) at Hannington
Public transport	Bus services between Newbury and Basingstoke stop at Kingsclere (excluding Sundays)

From picturesque Kingsclere, famed for its horse-racing stables, the walk heads up over Cottington's Hill to arrive at the hidden village of Hannington. From here it meanders through the lovely North Hampshire Downs, offering some great views over an area immortalised in Richard Adams's book *Watership Down*, before dropping back down to Kingsclere. A shorter walk misses out Hannington.

Kingsclere, once a royal manor, is home to **St Mary's Church**, which dates back to Norman times. Inside can be found a 12th-century Purbeck marble font, colourful stained-glass windows and the detailed 17th-century tomb of Sir Henry and Lady Bridget Kingsmill. The weather vane on top of the tower is known as 'The Bedbug'; legend has it that King John suffered from bedbugs while staying at a local inn.

In Swan Street, with St Mary's Church on the right, turn left up Anchor Road, passing the car park. At the top, where the road turns right, keep ahead up the enclosed

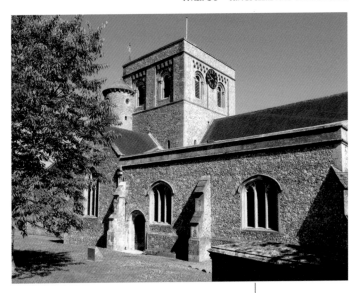

St Mary's Church, Kingsclere

path. Turn left along the track and then right to follow the right-hand side of the playing field; from the northern edge there is a good view of the downs.

Leave via a gate in the far-right corner and go down steps. Cross over Hollowshot Lane (track) and go into the field just left of the houses. Follow the right-hand hedge heading towards the mast on **Cottington's Hill**; the horse gallops are part of Park House Stables.

The Balding family are the current custodians of **Park House Stables**, a well-known horse-training establishment. During his time as head trainer, Ian Balding (father of TV presenter Clare Balding) trained many great winners including Mill Reef.

At the far-right corner go ahead into the trees. Turn left for 25m and fork half-right steeply up through the trees for 400m, crossing a stile mid way, to a path junction at the top.

Shorter route

Turn sharp right (west) for 250m, cross a stile and follow the fence on the left for 350m. Turn left over a stile and follow the fence up to a path junction. Turn right, and once in the next field turn left along the field margin to a junction. Turn right to rejoin the main walk (this point is indicated in the sidebar on page 182) and reach the B3051.

For the main route turn left and follow the line of Scots pines, then keep straight on, with the slope falling away to the left giving a great view across the Kennet Valley. Cross the stile at

the field corner and turn right up the track. Go straight on at the cross-track junction and follow the track alongside the field edge down to a dip and then up again, passing just left of the trees at Hannington Scrubs. Once in the next field turn left downhill and then right following the lower field edge. Go through a gate, turn left along the lane and keep right at the junction to reach the village green in **Hannington**. ▶

The peaceful village of **Hannington** huddles around the large village green, with its pyramidal-roofed well-head that was built to celebrate Queen Victoria's diamond jubilee. All Saints Church, which dates back to Saxon times, has two small windows engraved by Sir Laurence Whistler – one of which remembers William Whistler, whose family have farmed

The village green and well-head at Hannington

The Vine at Hannington pub is 200m straight on.

nearby for generations, and shows a scythe, sheaf of corn and flock of sheep.

Turn right alongside the green (left if coming back from the pub) and pass to the right of All Saints Church, following the gravel track towards Manor Farm. Before the entrance gate turn right along a signposted path, following it as it curves left round a barn, then keep to the enclosed path. Go through a gate and follow the enclosed track, then the left-hand undulating field edge. Enter the next field on **For Down** and turn right, following the right-hand edge for 600m. Bear left at the corner, still following the field margin, and at the next corner turn right past a gate to join Meadham Lane beside the entrance track for **Walkeridge Farm**. ◀

The lane here follows the Portway, a former Roman road between Sorviodunum (Old Sarum) and Calleva Atrebatum (Silchester).

Go left down the lane for a few metres and then right along the narrow enclosed byway following the Wayfarer's Walk, soon passing under power-lines. Once in the open field follow the field edge (grassy strip) down to the left, with views to the west along the sinuous chalk ridge, to reach a junction. ◀ Keep ahead to reach the B3051 at **White Hill** beside the car park (alternative parking/start).

The shorter route joins the main route here.

Cross diagonally left, pass a gate and follow the wide fenced track, signposted 'Wayfarer's Walk Inkpen Beacon 12½ miles', over **Cannon Heath Down**; to the right is a view across the deep hollow of The Warren. Continue for 1.7km to a gate in the fence on the right (SU 500 569); 500m straight on is the trig point on the top of **Watership Down**.

Watership Down has enjoyed almost legendary status since the author Richard Adams, born in Newbury, chose it as the setting for his best-selling story of the same name, based on the adventures of a group of rabbits.

Turn sharp right through the gate and head east-north-east across the gallop. Go through a gate and head east, parallel with the fence, for 400m before bearing

half-left steeply downhill, admiring the view on the way. Bear left through the trees and then turn right along the track for 375m. Turn left through a gap in the hedge and follow the grassy strip between fields heading north to join a gallop; bear right for 500m.

Turn right along the minor road towards **Kingsclere**, and at the junction turn right down Bear Hill. Cross the stream and bear left along Swan Street back to the church, passing the Bel & The Dragon pub and then a café; ahead, at the crossroads, is The Crown pub.

Following the Wayfarer's Walk around the deep hollow of The Warren

APPENDIX A
Route summary table

No	Start/finish	Start grid ref	Distance – km (miles)	Ascent (m)	Time (hrs)	Page
Berkshire Downs East						
1	Chapel Row	SU 571 696	11.6 (7¼)	230	3¼	22
2	Ashampstead	SU 565 769	6.9 (4¼)	65	2	28
3	Streatley	SU 567 812	8.8 (5½)	170	2½	32
4	Shillingford	SU 595 928	13.2 (8¼)	190	3¾	35
5	Blewbury	SU 530 860	13.7 (8½)	220	4	41
Lambourn Downs						
6	West Ilsley	SU 473 825	14.7 (9)	215	4	48
7	Ardington	SU 431 884	9.5 (6)	110	2½	53
8	Great Shefford	SU 383 752	14.4 (9)	290	4	58
9	Lambourn	SU 326 789	11.2 (7)	265	3¼	65
10	Sparsholt Firs	SU 343 850	12.5 (7¾)	225	3½	70
11	Whitehorse Hill car park	SU 292 865	11.9 (7½)	225	3½	74
12	Ashbury Folly	SU 273 843	10.4 (6½)	165	3	81
Marlborough Downs						
13	Ramsbury	SU 275 715	10.3 (6½)	165	3	86

No	Start/finish	Start grid ref	Distance – km (miles)	Ascent (m)	Time (hrs)	Page
15	Marlborough	SU 188 691	12 (7½) or 19.3 (12)	240 or 340	3½ or 5½	96
16	Ogbourne St Andrew	SU 190 721	20.6 (12¾) or 12.4 (7¾)	335 or 220	5¾ or 3½	103
17	Manton or Fyfield	SU 159 699 or SU 147 687	12.1 (7½) or 7.2 (4½); Fyfield add 2.5 (1½)	175 or 105; Fyfield add 75	3½ or 2; Fyfield add ¾	110
18	Overton Hill	SU 118 680	11.2 (7) or 11.5 (7¼)	165 or 205	3 or 3¼	115
Vale of Pewsey						
19	Smallgrain car park	SU 019 670	11.2 (7)	290	3¼	122
20	Smallgrain car park	SU 019 670	14 (8¾)	280	4	127
21	Near Alton Barnes	SU 115 638	14.8 (9¼)	340	4¼	133
22	Near Alton Barnes	SU 115 638	11.3 (7) or 6.4 (4)	270 or 130	3½ or 2	139
23	Martinsell Hill or Pewsey rail station	SU 183 645 or SU 160 604	13 (8) or 15 (9¼)	230 or 265	3¾ or 4¼	144
24	Great Bedwyn	SU 279 645	11.4 (7) or 8.5 (5¼)	200 or 160	3¼ or 2½	148
North Hampshire Downs						
25	Tidcombe	SU 290 582	9.7 (6)	220	2¾	154
26	Inkpen	SU 372 641	10.8 (6¾)	245	3¼	158
27	Ashmansworth	SU 415 574	9.5 (6)	280	3	164
28	St Mary Bourne	SU 421 503	7.6 (4¾)	100	2	169
29	Ecchinswell	SU 500 597	13.6 (8½)	290	4	173
30	Kingsclere	SU 525 586	12.8 (8) or 9.2 (5¾)	305 or 225	3¾ or 2¾	178

APPENDIX B
Useful contacts

Tourist information
Visit Hampshire
www.visit-hampshire.co.uk

Visit Newbury (covering West Berkshire)
www.visitnewbury.org.uk

Experience Oxfordshire
www.experienceoxfordshire.org

Visit Wiltshire
www.visitwiltshire.co.uk

Local information offices
Newbury
01635 30267

Swindon
01793 466454

Wallingford
01491 826972

Wantage
01235 760176

Public transport information
For train enquiries contact National Rail:

National Rail
03457 484950
www.nationalrail.co.uk

Traveline is the best resource for checking bus timetables:

Traveline
0871 2002233
www.traveline.info

Local Wildlife Trusts
Berks, Bucks and Oxon
Wildlife Trust (BBOWT)
01865 775476
www.bbowt.org.uk

Hampshire and Isle of Wight
Wildlife Trust
01489 774 400
www.hiwwt.org.uk

Wiltshire Wildlife Trust
01380 725670
www.wiltshirewildlife.org

Other contacts
North Wessex Downs AONB
01488 685440
www.northwessexdowns.org.uk

English Heritage
0370 333 1181
www.english-heritage.org.uk

National Trust
0344 800 1895
www.nationaltrust.org.uk

Ramblers Association
020 3961 3300
www.ramblers.org.uk

Animal Rescue
for sick, injured or distressed
animals or birds
RSPCA: 0300 1234 999

APPENDIX C
Further reading

Burl, Aubrey *Prehistoric Avebury* (Yale University Press; 2nd revised edition, 2002)

Cunliffe, Barry *Wessex to AD1000* (Longman, 1993)

Davison, Steve *The North Wessex Downs* (Robert Hale, 2013)

Greenaway, Dick *Around the Valley of the Pang* (Friends of the Pang, Kennet and Lambourn Valleys, 2007)

Leary, Jim and Field, David *The Story of Silbury Hill* (English Heritage, 2010)

Pevsner, Nikolaus (founding editor) The Buildings of England, series of guides split by county including Wiltshire, Oxfordshire, Berkshire and Hampshire (Yale University Press)

Smith, Esther *Savernake Forest: The Complete Guide to the Ancient Forest* (Forward Publications, 2010)

LISTING OF CICERONE GUIDES

Mountain Biking on the
  South Downs
Suffolk Coast and Heath Walks
The Cotswold Way
The Cotswold Way Map Booklet
The Great Stones Way
The Kennet and Avon Canal
The Lea Valley Walk
The North Downs Way
The North Downs Way Map Booklet
The Peddars Way and Norfolk
  Coast path
The Pilgrims' Way
The Ridgeway National Trail
The Ridgeway Map Booklet
The South Downs Way
The South Downs Way Map Booklet
The Thames Path
The Thames Path Map Booklet
The Two Moors Way
The Two Moors Way Map Booklet
Walking Hampshire's Test Way
Walking in Cornwall
Walking in Essex
Walking in Kent
Walking in London
Walking in Norfolk
Walking in the Chilterns
Walking in the Cotswolds
Walking in the Isles of Scilly
Walking in the New Forest
Walking in the North Wessex Downs
Walking on Dartmoor
Walking on Guernsey
Walking on Jersey
Walking on the Isle of Wight
Walking the Jurassic Coast
Walking the South West Coast Path
Walking the South West Coast Path
  Map Booklets:
  Vol 1: Minehead to St Ives
  Vol 2: St Ives to Plymouth
  Vol 3: Plymouth to Poole
Walks in the South Downs
  National Park

WALES AND WELSH BORDERS
Cycle Touring in Wales
Cycling Lon Las Cymru
Glyndwr's Way
Great Mountain Days in Snowdonia
Hillwalking in Shropshire
Hillwalking in Wales – Vols 1&2
Mountain Walking in Snowdonia
Offa's Dyke Path
Offa's Dyke Path Map Booklet
Ridges of Snowdonia
Scrambles in Snowdonia
Snowdonia: 30 Low-level and
  easy walks – North

Snowdonia: 30 Low-level and
  easy walks – South
The Cambrian Way
The Ceredigion and Snowdonia
  Coast Paths
The Pembrokeshire Coast Path
The Pembrokeshire Coast Path
  Map Booklet
The Severn Way
The Snowdonia Way
The Wales Coast Path
The Wye Valley Walk
Walking in Carmarthenshire
Walking in Pembrokeshire
Walking in the Forest of Dean
Walking in the Wye Valley
Walking on Gower
Walking on the Brecon Beacons
Walking the Shropshire Way

IRELAND
The Wild Atlantic Way and
  Western Ireland
Walking the Wicklow Way

**INTERNATIONAL CHALLENGES,
COLLECTIONS AND ACTIVITIES**
Canyoning in the Alps
Europe's High Points

AFRICA
Kilimanjaro
The High Atlas
Walking in the Drakensberg
Walks and Scrambles in the
  Moroccan Anti-Atlas

ALPS CROSS-BORDER ROUTES
100 Hut Walks in the Alps
Alpine Ski Mountaineering
  Vol 1 – Western Alps
  Vol 2 – Central and Eastern Alps
Chamonix to Zermatt
The Karnischer Hohenweg
The Tour of the Bernina
Tour of Monte Rosa
Tour of the Matterhorn
Trail Running – Chamonix and the
  Mont Blanc region
Trekking in the Alps
Trekking in the Silvretta and
  Ratikon Alps
Trekking Munich to Venice
Trekking the Tour of Mont Blanc
Walking in the Alps

**PYRENEES AND FRANCE/SPAIN
CROSS-BORDER ROUTES**
Shorter Treks in the Pyrenees
The GR10 Trail
The GR11 Trail

The Pyrenean Haute Route
The Pyrenees
Walks and Climbs in the Pyrenees

AUSTRIA
Innsbruck Mountain Adventures
The Adlerweg
Trekking in Austria's Hohe Tauern
Trekking in the Stubai Alps
Trekking in the Zillertal Alps
Walking in Austria
Walking in the Salzkammergut:
  the Austrian Lake District

EASTERN EUROPE
The Danube Cycleway Vol 2
The High Tatras
The Mountains of Romania
Walking in Bulgaria's National Parks
Walking in Hungary

**FRANCE, BELGIUM AND
LUXEMBOURG**
Chamonix Mountain Adventures
Cycle Touring in France
Cycling London to Paris
Cycling the Canal de la Garonne
Cycling the Canal du Midi
Mont Blanc Walks
Mountain Adventures in
  the Maurienne
Short Treks on Corsica
The GR20 Corsica
The GR5 Trail
The GR5 Trail – Benelux
  and Lorraine
The GR5 Trail – Vosges and Jura
The Grand Traverse of the
  Massif Central
The Loire Cycle Route
The Moselle Cycle Route
The River Rhone Cycle Route
The Way of St James – Le Puy to
  the Pyrenees
Tour of the Queyras
Trekking in the Vanoise
Trekking the Robert Louis
  Stevenson Trail
Vanoise Ski Touring
Via Ferratas of the French Alps
Walking in Provence – East
Walking in Provence – West
Walking in the Ardennes
Walking in the Auvergne
Walking in the Brianconnais
Walking in the Dordogne
Walking in the Haute Savoie: North
Walking in the Haute Savoie: South
Walking on Corsica

GERMANY
Hiking and Cycling in the
  Black Forest
The Danube Cycleway Vol 1
The Rhine Cycle Route
The Westweg
Walking in the Bavarian Alps

HIMALAYA
Annapurna
Everest: A Trekker's Guide
Trekking in Bhutan
Trekking in Ladakh
Trekking in the Himalaya

ITALY
Italy's Sibillini National Park
Shorter Walks in the Dolomites
Ski Touring and Snowshoeing in
  the Dolomites
The Way of St Francis
Trekking in the Apennines
Trekking in the Dolomites
Trekking the Giants' Trail:
  Alta Via 1 through the Italian
  Pennine Alps
Via Ferratas of the Italian Dolomites
  Vols 1&2
Walking and Trekking in the
  Gran Paradiso
Walking in Abruzzo
Walking in Italy's Cinque Terre
Walking in Italy's Stelvio
  National Park
Walking in Sicily
Walking in the Dolomites
Walking in Tuscany
Walking in Umbria
Walking Lake Como and Maggiore
Walking Lake Garda and Iseo
Walking on the Amalfi Coast
Walking the Via Francigena
  pilgrim route – Parts 2&3
Walks and Treks in the
  Maritime Alps

JAPAN, ASIA AND AUSTRALIA
Hiking and Trekking in the Japan
  Alps and Mount Fuji
Hiking the Overland Track
Japan's Kumano Kodo Pilgrimage
Trekking in Tajikistan

MEDITERRANEAN
The High Mountains of Crete
Trekking in Greece
Treks and Climbs in Wadi Rum,
  Jordan
Walking and Trekking in Zagori
Walking and Trekking on Corfu

Walking in Cyprus
Walking on Malta
Walking on the Greek Islands –
  the Cyclades

NORTH AMERICA
The John Muir Trail
The Pacific Crest Trail

SOUTH AMERICA
Aconcagua and the Southern Andes
Hiking and Biking Peru's Inca Trails
Torres del Paine

SCANDINAVIA, ICELAND
AND GREENLAND
Hiking in Norway – South
Trekking in Greenland – The Arctic
  Circle Trail
Trekking the Kungsleden
Walking and Trekking in Iceland

SLOVENIA, CROATIA, SERBIA,
MONTENEGRO AND ALBANIA
Mountain Biking in Slovenia
The Islands of Croatia
The Julian Alps of Slovenia
The Mountains of Montenegro
The Peaks of the Balkans Trail
The Slovene Mountain Trail
Walking in Slovenia: The Karavanke
Walks and Treks in Croatia

SPAIN AND PORTUGAL
Camino de Santiago:
  Camino Frances
Coastal Walks in Andalucia
Cycle Touring in Spain
Cycling the Camino de Santiago
Mountain Walking in Mallorca
Mountain Walking in
  Southern Catalunya
Portugal's Rota Vicentina
Spain's Sendero Historico: The GR1
The Andalucian Coast to Coast Walk
The Camino del Norte and
  Camino Primitivo
The Camino Ingles and Ruta do Mar
The Camino Portugues
The Mountains of Nerja
The Mountains of Ronda
  and Grazalema
The Sierras of Extremadura
Trekking in Mallorca
Trekking in the Canary Islands
Trekking the GR7 in Andalucia
Walking and Trekking in the
  Sierra Nevada
Walking in Andalucia
Walking in Menorca

Walking in Portugal
Walking in the Algarve
Walking in the Cordillera Cantabrica
Walking on Gran Canaria
Walking on La Gomera and El Hierro
Walking on La Palma
Walking on Lanzarote and
  Fuerteventura
Walking on Madeira
Walking on Tenerife
Walking on the Azores
Walking on the Costa Blanca
Walking the Camino dos Faros

SWITZERLAND
Switzerland's Jura Crest Trail
The Swiss Alpine Pass Route –
  Via Alpina Route 1
The Swiss Alps
Tour of the Jungfrau Region
Walking in the Bernese Oberland
Walking in the Engadine –
  Switzerland
Walking in the Valais
Walking in Zermatt and Saas-Fee

TECHNIQUES
Fastpacking
Geocaching in the UK
Map and Compass
Outdoor Photography
Polar Exploration
The Mountain Hut Book

MINI GUIDES
Alpine Flowers
Navigation
Pocket First Aid and
  Wilderness Medicine
Snow

MOUNTAIN LITERATURE
8000 metres
A Walk in the Clouds
Abode of the Gods
Fifty Years of Adventure
The Pennine Way – the Path,
  the People, the Journey
Unjustifiable Risk?

For full information on all our guides,
books and eBooks,
visit our website:
www.cicerone.co.uk

CICERONE

Trust Cicerone to guide your next adventure, wherever it may be around the world...

Discover guides for hiking, mountain walking, backpacking, trekking, trail running, cycling and mountain biking, ski touring, climbing and scrambling in Britain, Europe and worldwide.

Connect with Cicerone online and find inspiration.

- buy books and ebooks
- articles, advice and trip reports
- podcasts and live events
- GPX files and updates
- regular newsletter

cicerone.co.uk